Rosemary McCall is a lip-reading teacher of long experience, and a well-known writer and speaker on hearing loss in adult life. Having been in charge of an NHS audiology department for many years, she became increasingly concerned about the lack of assessment and assistance towards rehabilitation. This led to the formation of Link, the British Centre for Deafened People, registered as a charity in 1972. Among her numerous publications is the standard textbook *a word in your eye* and her booklet *Hearing loss – hearing aids*. Rosemary McCall lives in East Sussex.

By the same author

A word in your eye
I see what you mean
Are you someone else's ears?
Hearing loss – hearing aids
Communication barriers in the elderly
The effects of sudden profound hearing loss in adult life

Hearing loss?

A Guide to Self-help

ROSEMARY McCALL
Foreword by Lady Evelyn M. Templer

ROBERT HALE LIMITED
LONDON

Robert Hale Limited
Clerkenwell House
Clerkenwell Green
London EC1R 0HT

ISBN 0 7090 4393 7

Printed in Great Britain by
St Edmundsbury Press Limited, Bury St Edmunds, Suffolk
and bound by WBC Bookbinders Limited

Contents

concentrated on rhythm. Choice of practice partner (PP). Preparation for work with PP. Self-preparation for PP. Exercises with PP

Foreword

To lose, in adult life, and in full activity, one of the main channels of communication with others, is a crushing blow to professional and social life, though it must be equally painful, personally, at any age.

I have never understood why blindness arouses instant and universal sympathy and a desire to help: while to suffer a loss of hearing seems almost to cause hostility and avoidance of the sufferer. Speech is, after all, the main channel of communication between humans, and one would have expected the loss or partial loss of ability to hear speech to invoke sympathy and a desire to help.

Sadly, this idea does not seem to be the case very often, and I feel that this book may help people with hearing loss to make their circumstances better understood and to learn to overcome this hurtful indifference. It will equally help the partner and family, for whom hearing loss in a loved one can cause frustrating misunderstanding.

I have been privileged to know LINK, the British Centre for Deafened People, since its inauguration, and have been able to talk to many of its visitors – they are not patients, but guests – who have visited it, and who, with their families, have been helped by Miss McCall, the founder and Director of the organization. Miss McCall has already done much to help people with hearing loss to solve some of their problems, and I hope this book will have a wide readership among them, and all those who would like to help them.

LADY EVELYN M. TEMPLER
Life President, Commonwealth Society for the Deaf
Vice President Emeritus South-East Regional Association for the Deaf

Acknowledgements

Many teachers of lip-reading have urged me to write this book, but without one of them, Lena Butterworth, it would never have seen the light of day. It was her insistence that made me rise at 5.45 each morning! I quickly discovered how much I looked forward to these early hours and to writing without interruptions.

I am also extremely grateful to four friends: Raymond D'Ancey and Olga Hake, who both rely solely upon speechreading, Madge Thomson (a hearing-aid user), and Pamela Joy, all of whom read the script. It was in 1971 that Madge and Pamela shared with me the concept of starting LINK. From this beginning the British Centre for Deafened People emerged and an ideal became a reality.

I would also like to record my appreciation to the Community Health Council and to Soroptimist International (Eastbourne) for allowing me three months' leave from meetings.

My thanks, for their useful contributions, to H.K. Bonning, V. Crabb and Ray Jones.

Introduction: Sound Sense

It is estimated that ten million people in this country have impaired hearing.[1] Hearing loss is complex and personal but, whatever the type or degree of loss, it interferes with easy communication between people, which can be very exasperating. If you have suffered some hearing loss in adult life, this book is for you. It is about developing new skills and forming new habits, using sight and other assets in order to tackle the situation in a practical way. It is the outcome of many years of practical experience.

Lip-reading, literally understood, is a narrow concept. Speech-reading has wider implications. In broad terms it could be thought of as using sight as effectively as possible to aid communication; using experience of language, of speech and of people; developing the aural memory bank and awareness of the tactile sense; developing visual acuteness and above all alert mental perception.

Alexander Graham Bell invented the telephone as the result of trying to find a hearing aid for his wife. Mrs Bell was an experienced speechreader and in 1894 she gave a good description of the art:

> Speechreading is essentially an intellectual exercise, the mechanical part performed by the eye is entirely subsidiary. The aim of the speechreader should be to grasp the message as a whole and not to attempt to decipher it word by word or even sentence by sentence.

The telephone has world-wide acclaim, but Mrs Bell's comments about speechreading deserve to be much better known. Its use – like the use of the telephone – can greatly aid communication.

Sight can supplement hearing wonderfully and can also be used in circumstances where hearing aids are of little or no use. We begin by taking stock of the situation so that we can start with clear aims and realistic expectations. By recognizing and using many hidden assets, a great deal may be achieved through rightly applied self-help, a framework for progress is suggested in the second part of this book. The third part is just as important because it is concerned with practical application, with some of the stepping-stones and stumbling blocks to progress which are often unrecognized – for example, listening-tactics and social strategy, tension and tinnitus. There are some helpful hints for friends and family, too.

How much hearing is enough is a difficult question. The amount of hearing loss is not the same as the degree of handicap it causes. The book is written only for people whose hearing loss of any degree was acquired in adult life. Hearing loss is a very individual matter as you will see from the following four examples:

Mrs Brown is an active elderly lady who finds committee work increasingly difficult. She cannot always follow what goes on, particularly in a group. She sometimes misses what the local vicar or the rapid speaker at the WI says. Her family complain that the TV is too loud. She finds her slight hearing loss inconvenient and sometimes annoying.

George Smith is fifty, a successful salesman. He had 'ear-trouble' five years ago. Although it has cleared up, it caused a permanent, fairly severe hearing loss. A modern hearing-aid is invaluable; in fact for him it means business as usual, and he keeps a spare aid handy in case of emergencies. 'I couldn't live without it,' says George.

Lilian Snow is thirty-four. Her hearing has deteriorated gradually for ten years; the high-pitched sounds are most affected. Her hearing-aid is helpful only in certain circumstances. A buyer for an exclusive dress shop, Lilian finds the background noises make listening very hard work. Striving to hear makes her head-noises worse; tension rises almost to breaking-point. After a busy day she enjoys the peace of her own charming flat but is too exhausted to meet people. Lilian's social life is becoming increasingly restricted.

Arthur Jones, aged twenty-two, was a medical student when a car crash totally destroyed his hearing. Suddenly cut off from sound, no longer able to follow his chosen profession, unable to hear his family, friends and colleagues or to enjoy his hobby (he played the violin), he found the whole direction of his life changed dramatically overnight.

You will recognize at once that these people's lives are very differently affected by hearing loss. This book is for anyone with hearing loss, be it slight, severe or total which began in adult life. It is also for their friends.

Part One

Taking Stock of the Situation

1. The Challenge of Hearing Loss

The challenge of hearing loss is that it interferes with communication. It affects awareness of the general background sounds of life which are not always heard consciously. It also affects easy communication between people because it interferes with hearing speech.

Defining the problem

Defining a problem is half way towards tackling it; something vague and nebulous is daunting just because its size and shape are unknown. Once you take its measure, you can start to deal with it in a practical way. Be as well informed as possible about your own hearing loss. Also have your eyes tested regularly: new glasses may improve your viewing.

It is not at all easy to assess your own hearing. Many different factors are involved. When someone is talking, you may be testing how well he or she speaks rather than how well you hear. To measure hearing, a trained and experienced person is needed in an acoustically suitable environment.

Some people have hearing which is 'good' on one day and 'poor' on another. This may give the unfortunate and totally wrong impression that someone 'can hear when he wants to'. Some people who do not hear quiet sounds at all have an abnormal dislike of loud sounds; some people hear better in background noise, but the majority hear less well in noise. Some people hear the speaker's voice but cannot distinguish the words.

If you are interested in the hearing mechanism – how ears work –

the standard text book is *Hearing* by John Ballantyne, published by Churchill Livingstone. Another small booklet, *Hearing loss – Hearing aids* (published by the South East Regional Association for the Deaf), covers many points in less depth. The amount of hearing loss may be less important than the type of hearing loss and its effect on your life.

Know and list situations which are particularly difficult and then discover if there are ways round, over or through them. Chapter 11, 'Listening Tactics and Social Strategy', may suggest new ideas.

Hearing-aids and speechreading

Advice from an ear specialist is, of course, the first essential. If hearing cannot be improved and a hearing-aid has been recommended, it requires careful selection and fitting. Special skills are also needed to take an ear impression and produce the most suitable ear mould (there are many variations; the ear mould itself can change the aid's performance and alter its acoustic properties). In addition you will want to know how, when and where to use it; you may need some training in order to become accustomed to it, and you need to know where it can be maintained and repaired easily.

Hearing-aids are artificial; no invention equals the astonishing performance of normal ears. For some people aids give excellent results, for others they are better than nothing, and for a small minority they are useless. This is why it is unwise to generalize from a personal experience of hearing loss.

Hearing-aids improve, hearing changes, so do have the situation reviewed from time to time. It is sad to meet people who struggle on doggedly with a faulty or out-of-date hearing-aid because once, long ago, someone said they must persevere.

Sight and hearing together

When sight and hearing are used together, they are more effective than either used in isolation. Speechreading/lip-reading may provide that extra help to supplement the hearing-aid.

In contrast, some people find that using a hearing-aid makes speechreading more difficult. If it can only give a jumbled pattern of noise, this may be so distracting that it prevents concentration on the speaker and what he is saying. Head noises (tinnitus) may also interfere with concentration.

Speechreading unaided by any sound is very different from speechreading which is used to supplement and enhance the use of a hearing-aid. People who depend entirely on speechreading often become amazingly proficient.

Gradual or sudden hearing loss

If hearing loss is gradual, there is time to adapt and adjust to the situation, but there is also a real danger that hearing loss will lead to acceptance of unnecessary limitations. It is never too late to review and rethink.

The vast majority of adults who suffer hearing loss can be helped by amplified sound.

Sudden total deafness which is irreversible is very rare indeed. When the MP Jack Ashley experienced it, he said it was like 'drowning in a sea of silence'. A drowning man needs a lifeline quickly; his first objective is survival. Part of the survival kit is restoring communication. The right kind of assistance, including speechreading, should be available immediately. There is an organization in the UK, the Link Centre, which exists for deafened people and their families. It provides residential courses which are specially designed to meet individual needs in an environment of insight, love and understanding alongside professional assessment and assistance.

Points of view and some reasons for them

Other people may seem incredibly indifferent to the frustrations of hearing loss and unaware of the few simple ways to co-operate. Why is this?

People tend to take hearing for granted because it has been a continuous part of their life – starting even before birth. Without personal experience of hearing loss, there may be no instinctive understanding, no insight, to help them to co-operate. There is need for an imaginative and intuitive leap which some people seem unable to make. The crucial importance of 'hearing people talking' is rarely recognized. Indeed, I have met otherwise astute people whose comment about total hearing loss is, 'Such a pity not to hear the birds!'

It is worth reminding ourselves, too, that sound is invisible, and people cannot see someone not hearing or see how exasperating it is to mishear.

This lack of interest, lack of co-operation or plain indifference to hearing loss is caused by lack of insight and imagination. It calls for patience, tolerance and often self-control on your part; it helps to remember how difficult it is for some people to take the imaginative leap needed.

Attitudes are improving; television is increasingly influential; there is more enlightened concern than there was even a decade ago. You are likely to meet more and more helpful people, but there will always be some who cannot grasp the situation. Try to be patient with them.

'Why doesn't he say he hasn't heard?' This implies that, if only someone says 'I'm deaf', then the speaker will know what to do and will do it, and all will be well! However, there are good reasons why some people do not advertise their hearing loss.

It is not always possible to know when you have not heard something. It is not enough for the speaker to say, 'I told you aunty was coming on Monday.' Just because she has said so does not mean that you have received the message! Or again, how can you know that someone rang the bell if you didn't hear it ringing? How can you say you haven't heard something which in fact you didn't know about because you didn't hear it?!

At meetings a speaker may say, 'Will anyone who can't hear me please put up his hand.' I am always tempted to put up mine and ask, 'What did you say?'

What are they laughing at? You may know that people are talking but not what they are saying. If you see people talking or laughing together, it certainly looks interesting, but if you ask 'What's the joke?', they may say, 'Oh it doesn't matter' or, 'I'll tell you later', which leaves you in the dark. It may also infuriate you. To tell you later on does not give you the opportunity to contribute and join in; anyway, what *was* the joke?

The fact is that small talk and general chit-chat are not of world-shaking importance and therefore do not seem worth repeating – that is, if you already know what it is about. Seemingly trivial chatter can be thought a frivolous waste of time, unworthy of repetition, but the titbits of information and opinion add spice, colour and comment which reveal much about the speaker. In such chatter a word or two may be tossed about like a passing feather or bubble, and there is a spontaneous twinkle of laughter – a relaxed, amusing situation, but only if you hear what is going on. As a friend said to me, 'I don't want to have to wait for a world crisis in order to join in the conversation.'

People who are seen talking but who cannot be heard may look furtive, as if they are saying something which on no account must be overheard. They may not be as sinister as they look – give them the benefit of the doubt!

Recently I watched two women talking together at a bus stop. They glanced round from time to time, then drew closer and furrowed their brows. What were they planning? Were they professional shoplifters? Terrorists perhaps? Curiosity got the better of me. I sidled up behind them, and to my surprise they were saying that their feet were killing them and that flat shoes were better than court shoes.

Speechreading is not a cure for hearing loss, but it can be an important element within the overall plan. It is never an end in itself.

On the positive side, the last two decades have seen big advances; much research taking place, growing recognition of tinnitus; launch of the sympathetic hearing scheme; sophisticated surgery; developments in technology and a growing improvement in many spheres together with recognition that much can be done to improve matters.

List of professional roles

It will be useful to you to know the qualifications and duties of some professional workers who are involved with hearing impairment. This list was produced by the British Society of Audiology.

Audiology Technician (Physiological Measurement Technician – Audiology). A technician concerned with performing basic audiological tests and hearing-aid fitting will normally have completed the training and examinations specified by the Audiology Technicians Group of the British Society of Audiology. Higher grades undertake a wider range of specialized work relating to neurological and vestibular diagnosis and fitting of hearing-aids with basic rehabilitation procedures. (approx. 400-500 in UK.)

Hearing-aid Practitioner (Hearing-aid Dispenser). A person registered with the Hearing Aid Council as a Hearing-aid Dispenser to dispense aids in conformity with the provisions will have at least one year of service training and will have passed Hearing Aid Council qualifying examinations.

Hearing Therapist. A person within the NHS with specific responsibility for the rehabilitative care of hearing-impaired individuals, having completed a one-year training course.*

Otolaryngologist (ENT Surgeon, Otologist). A surgeon specializing in disorders of the ear, nose and throat who has successfully completed the seven-year course of postgraduate training prescribed by the Joint Committee on Higher Surgical Training. This description applies to a Consultant in Otolaryngology. Those still under training would be described as Senior House Officer, Registrar or Senior Registrar in Otolaryngology according to their status.

Social Worker for the Deaf. Generally a qualified social worker employed by the local authorities who has undertaken further training to deal with the specific problems of the prelingually deaf. Some social workers for the deaf also provide services for the hard of hearing.

Teacher of the Deaf. A qualified teacher who has undertaken further training leading to a certificate or diploma for Teachers of the Deaf. This training qualifies the teacher to work in special schools or special classes attached to ordinary schools, or to undertake peripatetic work with hearing-impaired children in ordinary schools.

Teacher of the Deaf (Audiology). A qualified teacher of the deaf who has undergone further training, usually leading to a postgraduate diploma or degree in audiology. They are employed usually by local authorities in the evaluation of hearing-impaired children, in the counselling of those children and their parents and as advisers on the provision of educational services for hearing-impaired children.

Audiological Scientist. Normally a graduate with a post-graduate qualification in audiology who is concerned with the performance and interpretation of sophisticated audiological and vestibular investigations and who has responsibility for establishing and monitoring scientifically based procedures for auditory assessments and rehabilitation, calibration and maintenance of audiometric equipment.†

Physician in Audiological Medicine (Audiological Physician). A physician concerned with the diagnosis, medical treatment and

---

* Annual training courses for a limited number of students have been held since 1978.

† This category, formed in the 1970s, has three grades; workers serve large regions rather than one hospital.

rehabilitation of patients with disorders of hearing and balance and who has completed successfully the seven-year course of postgraduate training prescribed by the Joint Committee on Higher Medical Training. This description applies to a Consultant Physician in Audiological Medicine; those still under training are described as Senior House Officer, Registrar or Senior Registrar in Audiological Medicine according to their status.

Senior Medical Officer (Audiology). A medical practitioner concerned with the primary audiological evaluation of children on a community basis will generally have the postgraduate training in paediatrics and audiology and will be employed by a District Health Authority.

In addition to the above list, produced by the British Society of Audiology, the Association of Teachers of Lipreading to Adults (ATLA) offers membership to anyone who has been teaching lipreading for two years, to students in training, and to those who have successfully completed a recognized training course to qualify them to teach lipreading to adults. Some speech therapists also now specialize in work with hearing-impaired people
    A lipspeaker repeats clearly (but silently) what is being said; the message is sometimes condensed or modified in more easily recognized words. Lipspeakers are not necessarily understood by all lipreaders.
    You will notice that professionally qualified workers are mainly in the field of diagnosis and treatment or their responsibility is with hearing impairment in children.

In conclusion three thoughts about communication

Communication does not happen in a social vacuum. Two essentials are somebody to talk to and something to talk about.
    Finally, two quotations.
    First, Einstein: 'Imagination is more important than knowledge.'
    Secondly, a message from Bram Taylor, not so well known as Einstein but someone who coped with sudden total deafness magnificently: 'Tell people,' he said, 'if you lose your hearing and want sympathy, you'd better develop a limp.'

2. Speechreading Aids Communication

Communication – people talking?

The aim of speechreading is to *improve communication in the ordinary situations of everyday living.*

If you ask several people to define communication, you will probably get a variety of answers. If they have not thought about the subject, they may reply 'It's people talking, of course.' Not so! You and I know that this is a totally wrong notion. Many people talk but their message is not received, let alone understood. To quote Joyce Grenfell: 'It takes more than the gift of tongues to communicate clearly!'

Communication is the sharing of thoughts, ideas, information and feelings so that they are understood. It is an intricate process which only succeeds if understanding takes place in the mind of the receiver. It is a partnership involving sender and receiver.

The speech chain

Communication is more than words, and it is more than speech. Much communication is visual. (We shall think about this in the important Chapter 5, 'See and Perceive'.) When people converse, they are creating a chain of events. Hearing loss affects No. 5 in the chain.

Even when hearing is perfect, there are often weak links in the chain. For example, it may not be possible to understand a mumbler, someone who uses unfamiliar language, jargon or technical terms. The sender may have difficulty in finding the right words to express himself; even when being transmitted the message may meet hazards such as constant interruptions and distractions, glaring lights, background noise, impossible acoustics and so on. How much easier to share an intimate chat when relaxed at home in an easy chair than when standing in a large bare hall where children are rushing round and dogs are untethered.

1	2	3	4	5	6	7
Thought	Encoded into speech	Spoken	Transmitted	Received	Decoded into thought	Understood

SENDER

Response

(process reversed)

RECEIVER

Both sender and receiver may be influenced by differences in age, culture or education and by emotional factors such as prejudice or preconceived ideas, feelings of superiority or inferiority, or states of mind such as anxiety, fear or shyness.

What has this to do with hearing loss? A great deal! When one link in the communication chain is weak, then it needs reinforcing, and the other links need strengthening to back it up.

There is more to tackling hearing loss than is generally recognized: speechreading, listening tactics and, above all, a mind trained to use effectively all the clues it receives from all sources (not solely from speech).

The five senses

The five senses are the generally accepted means of communication. When one sense is weak, once again we must do all we can to reinforce it and to use the others as effectively as possible.

The sense of touch is direct and uncomplicated. There is no mistaking the message of a hug or a slap.

Helen Keller could not see or hear. She said:

The hands of people I meet speak to me – some people are so empty of joy that when I clasp their frosty fingertips, it's like shaking hands with the north-east wind.

Some people have hands with sunbeams in them, when they shake hands it warms my heart.

Then there is the clinging touch of a child's hand. Some people's handshake is full of unspoken sympathy, a hearty handshake gives me real pleasure, a strong warm handshake is like a benediction.

Do you notice different kinds of handshake? Do they 'speak' to you?

Sight can aid communication in a special way, not only by the trained eye observing people but literally by helping us to 'see what they mean'.

When Jack Ashley TD MP totally lost his hearing, he said: 'The great British public fails to appreciate that deafness gives an added ability to evaluate individuals and to make a rapid assessment of people.' Because of hearing loss, Jack can 'see further'.

Three different functions: hearing, listening, understanding

In *receiving speech* there are three closely related activities which are not the same but are often confused.

1. *Hearing* is involuntary. If ears are in good working order, there is no choice. You cannot stop hearing whether or not you want to.

2. *Listening* is voluntary; you do it by choice. It is an activity of the mind which costs an effort of attention. It is hard work.

3. *Understanding* depends on being able to interpret the message correctly. Speechreading is closely interwoven with all three activities.

Active listening

Active listening is our foundation. We have already noticed that listening is a mental focus of attention.

Speechreaders are good listeners, they listen ACTIVELY.

*A*wareness – attention – anticipation

*C*oncentration

*T*imed (speedily grasping the message, speedily responding)

*I*ntuitive (ability to anticipate)

*V*ersatile and flexible

*E*ffective in using all clues from all the senses

Focus of attention is often one of the most difficult new habits to acquire. How easy it is to glance away momentarily – even to flick cigarette ash – and so lose the speaker's train of thought.

Intuitive ability helps you to anticipate what is likely in the circumstances. Knowing the subject, the circumstances and the speaker, you can think ahead to deduce what is sensible and possible – thus reducing the element of uncertainty.

The 'time factor' is important. In spite of gathering all possible clues, the process of interpretation naturally takes longer when there are fewer clues available from hearing. Spoken thoughts are produced in an envelope of time; if the process is abnormally slow or abnormally fast, this interferes with understanding the speaker.

Mental agility is needed to grasp the message speedily. Responding quickly to what is said helps to establish rapport, but repeating what is said slows down communication. The following are some examples of active and non-active listening.

Mr A: Which way to the station please?

Mr B: (Thinks. Replies) Which way ... (pause) ... did you want the railway station?

Mr A: Yes, yes the railway station.

Mr B: Ah – which way to the railway station? Well now ... (pause) ... the railway station ... (pause) ... let me see ... (pause)

Mr A: Thanks, thanks, never mind. (He then asks Mr C, who happens to be a speed speechreader and has already noticed the suitcase and Mr A's slightly flustered look.) Which way to the station?

Mr C: Railway station, first right, five minutes walk, bus station straight on past the traffic lights.

Mr A: Thanks a lot.

In the following example, two people are having an interrupted monologue. They both hear well but neither listens.

Her: Good morning. Lovely day. Did you have a good weekend?

Him: Lovely. Played golf, two rounds.

Her: Good. I went for a walk by the sea; it was very rough.

Him: Yes, I went to the Downs Golf Club.

Her: Oh, I met Mrs Brown by the pier.

Him: Mm. Well, I did the first round in seventy-eight.

Her: Really? Mrs Brown's dog had been run over.

Him: Ah! then I had a noggin in the club and met old Jones.

Her: Mrs Brown looked quite poorly really.

Him: Well, he wanted me to play another round so what could I say?

What a contrast when I met someone who had become totally deaf and blind in middle age.

He shook hands; he created immediate rapport. He asked me to write into his hand. He asked shrewd and stimulating questions. I was not surprised that many people came to him with their problems, trusted him with their thoughts and their worries. His secret? He 'listened' with attention and empathy. It was only afterwards that I discovered that he was the founder of the Deaf/Blind Helpers League.

Exercise on anticipation

Be aware of people; anticipate what they may say. Guess who said the sentences below: say each sentence aloud to yourself at normal speed, filling in the last word. For example: 'Lovely fresh fish, plaice was in the sea this morning, local caught. This was said by a ...' (Yes, it *was* a fishmonger.)

It is only the first time that you read the sentences that this exercise is effective, so read no further until you are ready to begin.

Say each of the following sentences at normal speed. Include the part which is shown by dots:
1. 'Buy a bunch of white heather dearie, only 10p a bunch, brings you luck,' was said by a ...
2. 'Open wide. I shan't hurt you,' was said by a ...
3. 'Let me feel your pulse; say 99. Put out your tongue,' was said by a ...
4. 'Sorry! Full up, there's another one behind,' was said by a ...
5. 'Would you come with me, sir? I think you might help us with our enquiries,' was said by a ...
6. 'Mind yer backs!' was said by a ...
7. 'I'm sorry to tell you that we are not able to provide a further loan,' was said by a ...
8. 'Time, gentleman, please,' was said by a ...
9. 'Have your tickets ready, please,' was said by a ...
10. 'Will all passengers fasten their seat belts, please,' was said by a ...

Learning to listen

Finally, a comment from Metropolitan Anthony Bloom:

> To be carried past one another in the street or in life, by the crowd or by chance, is not yet another encounter. We must learn to look and to see – to look attentively, thoughtfully, taking in the features of a face, its expression, the message of a countenance and of the eyes. We must learn, each of us and also in our human groups

social, political, racial, national, to see one another in depth, looking patiently, as long as necessary, in order to see who it is that stands before us.

Listening is an art we must learn, it is not words judged at their face value. We must listen with discernment to catch the thought that struggles to express itself, even tentatively, striving to make us aware of the treasures and agony of the heart ...

Such listeners are rare; they listen with mind and heart, even if their ears are not perfect. They are aware of the other person, not only of words.

Likely Speakers in Exercise on Anticipation
1. A gypsy. 2. A dentist. 3. A doctor. 4. A bus conductor. 5. A policeman. 6. A porter. 7. A bank manager. 8. A barmaid. 9. A ticket-collector. 10. An air hostess.

3. Changing Methods – Lip-reading and Speechreading

Recent developments

During the last few decades there has been stimulating rethinking about methods. If the 'whys and wherefores' are not for you, then you can skip most of this chapter with a clear conscience and join me again at the next section headed *Speechreading*.

Dr Robert H. Thouless, Reader in Educational Psychology and Fellow of Corpus Christi College, Oxford, suffered profound hearing loss. He then wrote a book, *Missing the Message*. An extract is as follows:

> If the lipreading deaf person has been properly taught he will have learned to interpret the *normal lip movements of ordinary conversation*; the distortion produced by exaggerated mouth movements will be unfamiliar and difficult to him. If, on the other hand, he were initially taught by means of such mouth movements, those of ordinary conversation would be unfamiliar and difficult to him. The aim of learning lipreading is to enable the deaf person to receive communication under ordinary everyday conditions, not to receive communication under special conditions adapted to the needs of the deaf.[2]

Our aim is 'to improve communication in *the ordinary situations of everyday living*'.

Recent research in the UK showed that tests of ability to distinguish isolated phonemes and syllables did not relate to tests of ability to discriminate normal, everyday speech in any meaningful way.

Some historic reasons for different methods are given by Jeffers and Berley (*Speechreading – Lipreading*, 1972): 'The belief that one could speechread through an additive approach undoubtedly stemmed from a confusion between speechreading/lipreading and speech development in the minds of the early teachers of deaf children who were also the first people to teach speechreading/lipreading to the hard of hearing ... the legacy of teaching in this fashion is still with us.'[3]

The majority of books on lip-reading have been written from the point of view of a teacher of deaf children. Almost all of them follow the 'part to whole' approach, from phoneme to syllable to phrase to paragraph.

The main sources of literature on teaching lip-reading came from the USA in the early part of this century and again in the 1930s. They were based on this analytical, additive method as being THE way.

When chatting in our mother tongue, we do not analyse each word but grasp the whole message; the sentence, not the word, is the unit of understanding. To concentrate on how isolated words are formed destroys the natural rhythm of speech; it directs attention to the 'mechanics' of speaking rather than to what is being said. The process which should be subconscious becomes conscious and interferes with understanding the speaker.

Adults who suffer hearing loss have assets not available to prelingually deaf children; above all, a lifetime using and hearing spoken language provides a 'memory-bank' of social/linguistic experience and expectation.

In the UK the value of analytical/additive method as an aid to communication is being questioned; it is not necessarily beneficial when applied indiscriminately to groups of people. Methods suitable for hearing-impaired children are totally inappropriate to people who have experienced a hearing loss as adults.

In 1953 D. Clegg, in *The Listening Eye*,[4] emphasized the importance of language experience; in 1961 O. Wyatt, in *Teach Yourself Lipreading*,[5] encouraged observation of the total person, including facial expression.

In 1972 my booklet *A Word in Your Eye*,[6] although a recognized text book, omitted the word 'lip-reading' altogether. It included use of the sensation of speech and making best use of social environment.

The social/environmental aspect was further explored in Denmark[7] and subsequent research resulted in *Hearing Tactics* (editor Svend Vognsen, 1976).

In the 1970s two books were published in Australia: *By word of mouth*, by Pat Pengelley,[8] which uses the sensation of speech in addition to the sound and appearance of speech, and *The Baker's Dozen*,[9] by Iris Regan and Dot Kellett, which stimulated visual activity, mental assimilation and quick response.

There have been some schools of thought in the UK which recommend total emphasis on training residual hearing through amplified sound and auditory training. The value of effective, appropriately taught speechreading is perhaps underestimated and overlooked.

Speechreading/Lip-reading – some general principles

Speechreading is not a magic formula which gives instant understanding of everything that everyone is saying all the time! However, other people may not always realize this.

Recently I interviewed a couple. 'My wife,' he said, 'must learn lip-reading.' A brief test revealed that she was already proficient. 'But,' he said, 'when she is doing her tapestry, she doesn't get a word I say.' We explained to him that, having only one pair of eyes, she needed to know that he was talking in order to look at him instead of looking at her tapestry.

People may forget that, although hearing is selective, sight has different attributes. Sight is limited to what is in front of your nose; you cannot be expected to see round corners or through walls, and no one can see in the dark.

Success in speechreading depends on more than acquiring skill. It is affected by opportunity, circumstances and other people. If you are feeling fit, alert and ready for anything, you will succeed better than when you are tired, 'off colour', worried, unhappy, tense or simply bored by the speaker.

How long will it take to learn? This is rather like asking how long it will take to learn to paint a picture. People vary; some have more natural aptitude than others. The amount of encouragement and co-operation they receive also varies.

Because speechreading is phonetic (it has no connection with spelling or written words), you can use it in any language, dialect or accent that is already familiar. Naturally some languages are easier than others because of their different characteristics, and you must know in advance which language is being spoken in order to put your memory bank into the 'right gear'. A linguist who has lost his hearing tells me that French and Spanish are the easiest languages for him to speechread. German is more difficult. So is Chinese, but that is something you are not likely to worry about.

Because speechreading demands intense concentration, it does not allow the luxury of half listening. The unwavering attention required is very hard work; your aim must be 'little and often'. Take one step at a time. Like any skill, it grows as you 'learn by doing'.

Speechreading offers many advantages. In addition to improving communication, it increases mental agility, visual acuity and powers of concentration. It can be invaluable to the hearing-aid user and a lifeline when hearing-aids are limited or useless. It also increases awareness of other people. At the very least, it costs nothing and is always with you (there is no risk of it getting lost, chewed by the labrador or falling into the bath).

Some people reach the stage when what is seen can be directly connected to their memory-bank of experience of spoken language. What is seen is perceived by the 'mind's-ear' and is almost like 'hearing through your eyes'. This stage is usually reached suddenly as an intuitive leap made at a subconscious level.

There is no doubt at all that speechreading is worthwhile, and you can start today, just where you are.

Speed Speechreading

Over the years I have met thousands of people who have suffered hearing loss as adults. It did not take long to discover that some were excellent speechreaders but had received no formal instruction; others had received instruction – sometimes for years – and, although theoretically faultless, it did not help them much in daily living.

I was particularly interested in the excellent speechreaders who were self taught. They followed normal conversation but could not follow slow, deliberate speech. How did they do it? What was their secret? One thing was obvious. They had used and developed their natural assets in a way which was undoubtedly effective.

'Lip-reading' literally means reading lips. But this natural method was different and was better described as 'using every clue as an aid to comprehension'. The 'natural method' people could not follow what was said if the speaker's eyes were covered. Without exception they were alert and observant; they followed normal speech at normal speed, but if the rhythmic pattern of the sentence was destroyed, then they could not follow what was said. Most certainly their success depended on something far beyond interpreting lip movements. That is why I call this natural method 'speed speechreading'.

People with normal hearing do not hear every word in order to understand, although they may not be aware of the extent to which their mind fills in the gaps. The telephone, for example, has a severe high-frequency cut; some sounds simply are not transmitted by the system, but only when there is no context, no 'language sense' to help, must the word be spelt out. 'No, not P for Peter but T for Tommy. Yes, S for sugar not F for Freddy,' and so on. If the subject is known the mind can anticipate, which, together with experience of language, carries us over many unnoticed 'gaps'.

Using assets – developing new habits.

The 'man in the street' is not necessarily an observant person; however, some people, for example the policeman or the artist, have become observant in a particular field. Their eyes are trained. Speed speechreaders have also trained themselves to observe.

Watching the speaker, even looking at his face, may be a habit to be cultivated before it becomes automatic. The ability to concentrate intently but not to strain can be developed, also the 'synthetic' ability to notice the rhythmic pattern of whole sentences, to grasp the meaning from a few clues.

Speed speechreading is natural, not something new or 'abnormal'. Your ingrained knowledge of speech and language provides a memory-bank of experience ready to be used. Speed speechreaders develop new skills of alert, concentrated attention, increase awareness and observation and apply the mixture with confidence and lack of tension.

This general framework is very different from the lip-reading 'textbook' approach, which at its most extreme consisted of pupils sitting in rows, dominated by a teacher and concentrating on the exaggerated formation of isolated sounds.

Although speechreading is natural, the pattern for progress within the general framework depends on the individual's aptitude and on the habits he has formed.

If hearing loss is gradual over many years, an individual may hardly notice that, almost imperceptibly, sight is taking over more and more responsibility as hearing becomes less effective. This is often an automatic and unconscious process, and good speechreading foundations are laid. No further training may be needed.

However, the opposite may happen. Unless sight is used in this positive way, the habit may be formed of concentrating harder on hearing as much as possible to the exclusion of everything else, particularly to the exclusion of sight. As hearing deteriorates, this person strains even harder to hear more; he may, in fact, make less use of his sight than someone who has normal hearing. If his hearing deteriorates to vanishing-point, his stumbling-block to progress may be this wrong habit of straining after sound.

A child told repeatedly 'It's rude to stare' may grow up reluctant to look at the speaker. In spite of his intellectual acceptance that to look at a speaker with polite interest is welcomed, and not a stare of hostility or inquisitiveness, in his subconscious mind the barrier lingers.

A different 'technical hitch' held back Mr X, whose lack of progress was causing me concern. He was a teacher with sudden severe hearing loss. He immediately read all the books about lip-reading he could find; he studied the theory of how spoken sounds were made; he was literally 'word perfect' and practised separate words diligently for hours. His progress in communication was almost nil.

One day, in desperation, I decided on a daring experiment. I disagreed with him on a controversial subject. As usual, much had to be written down. He became very annoyed and put forward arguments; I put forward counter-arguments; we were going 'ding-dong', hammer and tongs. He suddenly stopped in his tracks and said, in utter amazement, 'I'm *understanding* you!' A thrilling discovery. For the first time he had been thinking about what I was saying and replying to it instead of analysing every movement of every word. Now he was communicating – discussing a subject he knew well and felt strongly about. His whole mind was on the argument, and there was not time to wonder if he could and if so how he did. As in many skills, the pattern of progress is not a continuous, gradual increase of ability but there is a period of slow groping and suddenly part of the system works.

A skilled and experienced therapist may spot such stumbling-blocks to progress and suggest the way forward.

Learn by doing.

How do you start?

Acquiring a new skill may depend on the right guidelines, on using experience, imitation, repetition, recall; above all on LEARNING BY DOING.

Children learn skills such as swimming and speaking their native language at an early age. Their skills have not been acquired by careful intellectual considerations such as knowledge of water buoyancy or the rules of grammar. They *learn by doing*. The speed speechreader also *learns by doing*.

People with no hearing loss often have natural ability to speechread. Some people say, 'I hear better when I wear my glasses.' You, too, can start speed speechreading through *learning by doing*.

The principles are simple: developing your natural ability, using your assets, forming new habits.

The following comments are by two people who rapidly began to acquire speed speechreading. Their skills still need to be reinforced and extended, but the general principles are the same: they use assets they already possess. Both look attentively at the speaker; alert but not tense, they are thinking about the message being conveyed, using their mind to grasp the speaker's thought. The second example has also discovered the use of aural memory.

And on the third day – a moment of revelation at the Link Centre. By V. Crabb

A most exciting thing happened to me and my deafened husband today; suddenly we could converse effortlessly.

In order to allow this revelation to occur, I had had to eliminate pre-conceived ideas and established patterns of lip-reading. The wrong habits had become established because, as is often the case, my husband's hearing loss had been gradual and progressive. This meant that a slight increase in the volume of my voice overcame the problem initially, and that, as hearing worsened, greater care with articulation, coupled with a raised voice, enabled me to be understood.

It was not surprising, therefore, that increased deafness should produce increased effort on my part along the lines which had hitherto been successful, i.e. speak even louder (useless), articulate more emphatically (unnatural).

This progression in the wrong direction was halted, thanks to sessions of rapid speechreading at the Link Centre. Suddenly the concept of 'natural speech' in complete sentences dawned on both my husband and myself.

To us, the message came over on the following lines: relax; sit back; allow the natural rhythm of speech to take over. If one word is missed, don't repeat that word alone. Go back to the beginning of the sentence, even though this part has been fully understood. In this way, one can swing into the flow of the sentence, the rhythm of the comprehended words carries the difficult ones into the flow, and the recipient seems to pluck the meaning from his memory-bank as being the one most likely for the context. You find yourself thinking, 'How could it possibly mean anything else?'

The initial secret seemed to lie in beginning each sentence with the same few words – to establish the flow. Our skill is newly acquired, so I introduce each topic of conversation with an established phrase, taken from a limited range and related to a recent event where possible. Already we find that we can add to this range of opening lines considerably, using a known fact or phrase; the introduction sets the rhythm for the rest of the sentence, which then follows naturally.

The realization has been dramatic; we feel that we can't practise enough – to show off our new rapport – and delight in its success.

Now that we know we can do it, we can enjoy building up our range of tricks.

I look forward to having secret conversations across a crowded room!

Some observations about using aural memory – 'hearing in the mind's ear': by Ray Jones

I have been deaf for three months. The first month after my accident I was in hospital. The first month it was difficult to communicate with people, even though the doctors and nurses were very helpful.

The problem was I had become suddenly deaf, and looking at the face and movement of the lips and tongue did not mean a thing to me. The first week most things were written down for me, but this made me feel incapable, which I did not like.

So I asked everybody to speak first, and if I could not understand, then to write it down, and I found I could speechread quite well.

But I still missed a lot. Then, about two weeks after being in hospital, my best friend came to see me. We were speaking for about half an hour, and I had no trouble in understanding what he said. At first I thought I was hearing him, but I knew I could not be; what I was doing was putting the voice I knew with his lip movement, and it made all the diference.

This I experienced with everyone I had heard before I went deaf.

This still left a bit of a problem with strangers, until I came out of hospital. I went into a strange pub; the barman was small, plump and round-faced with a big smile, just like Harry Secombe. When he spoke first, it was obvious that he said, 'Yes, sir, what would you like?' After a little while I said, 'What have you got to eat?' He turned his back, looked at the rolls and sandwiches and was saying something. I told him I was deaf but that I could lip-read him. That's when we got talking. I just assumed that he sounded like Harry Secombe, and we had a good natter.

After that I found that, if I put a voice to the person, it was much easier to understand: important voices for authority, understanding voices for doctors, nurses and people like that, just a voice to suit the person.

In whatever way the individual ingredients are mixed, speed speechreading is based on natural assets already present, and on forming new helpful habits.

As you learn by doing, your subconscious mind absorbs gradually and becomes a trusted ally. This is more easily achieved when the process is enjoyable and interesting, and if you stop before you are tired. It is less easy and may be prevented altogether if you are anxious, strained or tense.

Part 2

The Way Forward

4. See and Perceive

Observation and awareness

Eye training, observation and awareness are first steps, using eye and mind together, being alert to other people and alive to the world around.

We all see – but an enormous amount of what is seen is not noticed; it does not register unless it is observed. The detective, the diamond merchant and the antique-dealer are trained to observe different things. You, too, need to become observant in a special way.

Watching should be alert but unforced, taking in everything calmly and without straining. This is not at all the same thing as staring with unblinking fixation.

For many people the most difficult initial stage is forming this habit of alert, easy watching. Sit back comfortably, not on the edge of your chair. Allow what you can see to *come to you*; do not feel you are 'chasing out' after it. Foster this habit of alert but unstrained attention. Observe people talking, the total person, the whole face and expression; notice the lips.

You can start whenever you are within eye-shot of other people; waiting in the post office, outside school when collecting the children, in the café, the train, the bus queue, waiting for your library ticket or the cat's fish. No longer are these minutes wasted or idled away: you are learning from watching people as they talk, noticing the pauses, the slight emphasis, the rhythmic flow of movements.

Notice general impressions. Does one person dominate or is it a mutual exchange? Are they animated, excited, bored, angry, interested, in agreement?

It so happens that I am writing this in the train. Not far off, two smartly dressed gentlemen both in city clothes are talking to each other. The man with his back to me is dominating; although I cannot see what he is saying, I see the face of his companion, the receiver. His eyes are searching the speaker's face; he eagerly hangs on every word; now and then he prompts with a question. He does not comment himself; he gives only enthusiastic affirmative answers. He is anxious to impress, not to 'put a foot wrong'.

In a more formal situation, facial expression is more likely to be controlled, even to be assumed. People may not want to reveal their thoughts and may acquire a poker face.

Your bank manager may greet you cordially. When the conversation gets round to your request for an overdraft, a slight but immediate narrowing of the eyes may indicate his decision long before he has begun to tell you about the 'present financial climate, the need for stringent measures, the inadvisability of raising false hopes, the realization of the need, the sincere regret' and so on. Being observant, you were pretty sure the answer would be no, anyway, before the explanation began.

Eye contact

Eye contact should not be lost when you speechread. People who avoid looking at the speaker may cause him a feeling of unease. What is he trying to hide? Why can't he look me in the face? To look at the speaker with attention is not only polite, it also encourages good communication.

When people meet, eye contact is often the first step towards communication. Instinctively you 'catch his eye'. 'Nice to see you' is more than a figure of speech.

Have you noticed people jammed together in a London rush-hour? Eye contact is avoided. At such close quarters eye contact would give personal recognition, allowing an unwelcome intrusion, a violation of privacy. There is a physical distance that is normally maintained between people. By avoiding eye contact, the stranger next to you is more easily regarded as a 'thing' than as another human being far too close for comfort; even if the stranger's elbow is jammed into your ribs and his suitcase bumps your shins, eye contact is avoided.

In conversation occasional eye contact is part of the ordinary 'feedback' process, which helps you to know the other person's reaction to what you are saying. Eyes meet to verify the truth of what is being said (is it factual? is there a twinkle in the eye?), that what you are saying is receiving attention, that you are seeing 'eye to eye'.

Dark glasses restrict communication even when people have no hearing loss. There is no doubt that they greatly limit speechreading.

Friend or foe?

Some speed speechreaders tell me that their eye focus is roughly on the speaker's nose but that at the same time they are acutely aware of eyes and lips.

It is natural to look away when searching for the right word or whilst racking one's brains. You will gradually train yourself to think and to look at the other person simultaneously.

Concentrate hard and think fast but do not use this mental activity to make you frown or glare at the speaker. An intense, strained expression gives the impression of anxiety, even of aggression which may make the other person vaguely uneasy. It helps to feel, and therefore to look, friendly; to regard the other person with genuine interest and attention because you like and enjoy his company.

It is tempting to get close to the speaker in order to hear him better but it requires distance between you for you to see the whole face and expression (noticing the lips). Too close, and your eyes can only focus on a few teeth, which won't tell you much. An optimum space between the speechreader and the speaker is at least four or five feet.

The unspoken language of non-verbal signals

Non-verbal signals (NVS) are conveyed by facial expression, movements, natural gestures, posture, distance, and so on. They vary with different nationalities and social groups.

In Latin races speech tends to be reinforced to a greater extent by NVS than in the cooler northern climates. In the United Kingdom it is traditional not to show one's feelings. Control of expressing emotions spontaneously is taught to children as part of their cultural upbringing and social development. A certain understatement and stiff upper lip sometimes puzzle and even exasperate foreigners.

Drake did not show alarm; he finished his game of bowls. Nelson played it cool; Churchill did not 'flap'.

In recent years there has been a tremendous upsurge of interest in NVS, and many books are available on the subject. This literature points out that just one look can convey a great deal – it may imply liking, sympathy, understanding, domination, comfort, even messages such as 'keep quiet' or 'not in front of the children'. The badges people wear can give clues about their interests and allegiances – it can even be a sign of insecurity that they need lots of badges to convince themselves that they 'belong', are 'OK people'.

The whole person 'speaks'; before he opens his mouth something has been conveyed to you.

Run me over, if
you like

Run me over, if
you dare

Awareness of the speaker

Words cannot always be taken at face value. A trained observer will know that 'what she said' is very different from 'what she felt when she said it'. Sometimes words taken literally can be misleading, particularly if you cannot assess the tone of voice which may convey the real meaning.

Below is a quotation from 'Seeing is believing' one of the many observation papers written for LINK, the British Centre for Deafened People.

What would you make of the mother who crossly says to her child, 'Of course I love you, don't be stupid.' Or the company chairman who listens to a speech with a bland smile in spite of an irritated foot tapping under his chair. Have you known a husband call up to his wife, 'No, dear, I'm not getting impatient', while swinging his car keys furiously round and round. The observant person will not be in the least surprised when the storm bursts – the child cries, the chairman votes against the proposal, and the husband, in a vile temper, swipes the gatepost.

What might be behind the clenched teeth, the drumming fingers, buttoning and unbuttoning a coat, fists clenched boxer-style, the raised eyebrow? How might the direction of a person's glance give clues to what he is thinking or feeling?

Self-training for perception

There are many ways to train your eye to observe and your mind to perceive. You may like to try some of the following suggestions.

Next time you are on a bus or train ... Notice one physical characteristic (i.e. a feature, movement, habit, etc) of at least six different people.

You visit someone's house ... Afterwards, can you make a rough sketch of the sitting-room? Where was the furniture? What colour were the curtains? What was on the mantelpiece? Was there a clock? A vase of flowers? Was there a path? Gravel? Cement? Paving? Mud with puddles? Straight from the street? Any notices about beware of the dog or bell out of order?

On a ten-minute walk ... Observe all the car stickers you see; what do they reveal about the car owner? Here are a few. 'Preserve Wild Life', 'Joggers of the world unite' and, on the back window of an ancient Austin, 'I may be old but I'm in front of you.'

Where are you reading this book? Trace back (from now) your activities for the hour before you started reading.

List the symbols you notice – what do they convey? Can you recall the symbols for the following?

1. Volkswagen
2. Transworld airlines
3. *Daily Express*
4. Pure wool
5. Oxfam

Do you know the symbols for: Shell petrol/diesel fuels, Philips (electric), the Royal Society for the Protection of Birds?

Pelmanism. Place a pack of cards face downwards on the table, either in neat rows or higgledy-piggledy. Turn over two cards and look at them; turn them face down; visualize what you saw and where they are in relation to the other cards. Repeat the process with other cards. When you have two of a kind (two queens, sevens, aces and so on), take them off the table. How long before all the pack is gathered in? Does your time decrease as your observation and visual memory increase?

Spot the difference between two pictures which are almost identical but have very small differences; these pictures often appear in cheap puzzle magazines from newsagents – not to be despised because they are enjoyed by children.

Kim's Game. Someone else should prepare twenty small objects on a tray which is covered with a cloth. Take off the cloth, look at the objects for one minute, cover the tray again and list the objects you can remember. (Three minutes.) Then remove the cloth again and check your list. Repeat this, with different objects, of course. You will find that your observation speed increases.

Glance at the shapes below for a few moments; look away while a friend covers one of them. Look again and try to draw the missing shape.

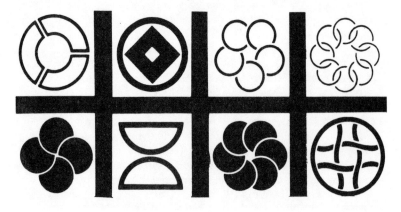

Here are two true stories about awareness and the lack of it.

The factory was five minutes walk from the canteen. A path linked them, and every day two hundred people walked along it from the factory to the canteen and back again. A questionnaire was given to the employees asking what they noticed along the path. Not one of them had seen the tall flowering cherry tree although part of it actually overhung the path.

One winter evening I went to a party. I arrived late and the room was full, everyone was talking. I made my way to a big picture window. The garden outside was floodlit, and the rain was teeming down. One other person was looking out of the window. I smiled and said, 'Good evening, isn't it wet!' (This seemed a non-controversial statement of fact as a good opening gambit.) To my surprise he replied, 'Why do people want diamonds when they can see the rain?' I looked again. The floodlight caught the raindrops which formed a continous shower of diamonds. I looked at the people in the room, chatting away. 'Do you think they know?' I asked him. He thought for a moment, then replied, 'Perhaps they are only half-alive.' Are you?

Experience has shown that speechreading training that is broadly based reveals new horizons, even new dimensions of living. By increasing your powers of observation and training your eye, you become more aware of and alert to other people and more deeply alive to the world around you.

May this brief chapter provide you with a few signposts upon an interesting journey which will certainly improve your speechreading skills.

5. Seeing Sounds

You have now become an *active listener*, your sharp eye noticing much that other people miss, combining alert observation with intense concentration.

People talk in sounds, not single words

You noticed the person doing the most talking; did you also notice the effect on the other person? The glazed look of boredom as he shifts from foot to foot; the encouraging smile of agreement and the well-placed question; the slight tightening of the lips and change of expression when there is disagreement; the ding-dong argument where both people talk at once; the impatient chipping-in with their own point of view while someone is still open-mouthed in mid-sentence.

You observed the whole face and expression, eyes and lips. You noticed that people talk in 'fits and starts'. Even the most voluble have to pause sometimes to take breath!

People talk in sounds. Part of the process which happens when they do it can be seen.

There is a rapidly moving rhythm and pattern to speech; the whole face may be animated or passive; lips and mouth are revealing; small movements of the jaw or an occasional small twitch of the double chin are part of the 'moving picture' of speaking.

In everyday speech, words are not produced in isolation and then strung together like beads on a necklace. Far from it. A fleeting sound may provide the end of one word and also the beginning of the next. Some words get crushed together or are swallowed up or even disappear completely. To break up the sentence destroys the natural rhythm. The sentence is a complete utterance in time, with a particular pattern and rhythm.

Do not look for individual words, which may not be there anyway; observe the movement, rhythm and pattern of the sentence as a whole in order to grasp the meaning. You can see some of the sounds as they are spoken. Use them rather like stepping-stones over a river. If you look for single words, you will never reach the far bank.

Sound, appearance, sensation (SAS)

Here is a spoken sentence. It looks and sounds like: 'Smorning slarmwen toff twirly.' (Of course the sounds which the speaker makes have no neat little spaces in between.) If you *see/hear/feel* the sentence as you say it, there is no problem in understanding it. Say it aloud at normal speed a few times to prove it. 'Hear' the voice mentally.

The same sentence written down would read, 'This morning's alarm went off too early', but single words are not what you *see/hear/feel* when someone speaks normally.

Now say the sentence again whilst you look at your face in a large mirror. Say it out loud at normal speed and notice what the sentence *looks* like. You will *hear* the sound (either through physical hearing or in your 'mind's ear') and you will also feel the movement of the whole sentence as you say it.

You will concentrate on sound/appearance/sensation (SAS for short), and you will learn by doing, using the threefold rope of SAS to cross the river.

Form a habit.

You will need to be alone, uninterrupted, and to look into a large mirror. A triple dressing-table mirror is ideal. Not everyone you wish to speechread will be exactly facing you when they speak; the two side flaps of a triple mirror allow you to see moving speech from several different angles including side face and three-quarter face.

Below are some everyday sentences to start you off. Use each one at normal speed, in exactly the same form, several times.

First, notice the overall pattern of the whole sentence as you say it. Secondly, associate in your mind the appearance with the sound (or memory of sound) as you say the sentence. Thirdly, associate in your mind the sound, appearance and sensation (the movement you *feel* when you say the sentence).

Good morning. What do you think of the weather?
Please can you tell me the time?
What part of the world do you come from?
When's your birthday?
Would you mind posting the letter for me?

Would you prefer tea or coffee?

Concentrate on this *sound/appearance/sensation* practice for only short periods at a time but several times a day. It is wasting effort to go on until your mind wanders and your concentration flags.

The object of this type of exercise, with its constant repetition of the same familiar sentence at speed, is to develop subconscious recognition of sentences as a whole unit, using the *sound/appearance/-sensation* input of natural speech. Successful speech-reading is not a conscious process. Its development is based on what you have already been doing all your life when talking yourself and when listening to other people talk. Your past experience is extended to strengthen the three strands of sound (or memory of sound)/appearance/sensation, combined with your ability to 'put two and two together'.

Once this threefold link is established, there can be more adventurous advances from firm foundations, the fundamental aim being to grasp the meaning of the sentence as a whole at normal speed.

You will quickly recognize what is already familiar; by forming the habit of responding quickly to the message the sentence conveys, you are immediately ready for the next comment from the other person. Speechreading is already helping towards communication.

The sentences I suggested all need a reply; if any of them are said as you go about your business, you will immediately recognize them and reply.

SAS drill

Try the following sentences for SAS drill in your learn-by-doing practice time. Remember, you are becoming aware of the pattern and rhythm of each sentence and noticing differences. You are learning by doing, not by thinking about it. Use SAS all the time. Say each sentence several times at normal speed, then repeat in random order.

A. Where do you live?
   What did you have for breakfast?
   What can you see out of the window?
   Is there a television set in the room?
   Is lunch at twelve o'clock or one o'clock?
   Which way to the sea front?
   Will you be walking all the way home?

Did you notice that there was something slightly different about the fourth sentence? What was it? Run through them again, at normal speed (each sentence as a total unit), and make the discovery.

Here are some further unconnected sentences. Each has a pause somewhere, so you will SAS two short total units, with a pause between.

B. If you're going home / can I come with you?
   When you go to the post office / will you buy me some stamps?
   You're awfully wet / where's your umbrella?
   The shops are shut / is Wednesday early closing?
   When can you pop in / there's always a welcome.
   Can you stop for tea / the kettle's boiling.
   Will you walk home / or would you rather wait for the bus?

I wonder if you noticed that in the last-but-one sentence something is missing that is in the other sentences. (It is the same slight difference that you noticed in sentence 4 of Group A.) Well, well, well, – why not work through this again.

Further examples of everyday sentences follow. Again, each should be SAS as two total units, with a pause between, and said aloud at normal speed.

It's slippery out / mind how you go.
It's past my bedtime / I'm off.
It's a pity you can't stop a bit longer / I'll see you out.
It's started to rain / get the washing in.
It's in the house somewhere / can you find it?
It's been a busy day / I'm all in.

You will notice that the very beginning of the sentence doesn't really matter at all. It's the pattern and rhythm that you depend on, seen and experienced as a whole.

Much later on, you might get your practice partner to say the first part of each sentence, while you immediately reply with the second part. This is utterly useless unless your practice partner can speak in normal up-to-time speech; slow down or exaggerate and the vital links you are building will be broken. Far better no practice partner at all than the wrong one, however eager. On no account look for one until you have finished this chapter.

Think of everyday short sentences yourself, forget the words, think of the Sound (or memory of sound), Appearance and Sensation of the complete unit.

The next step forward is to keep the first part of the sentence the same but change the second part. For example:

Where on earth are my gloves? / They're on the floor.
Where on earth are my gloves? / They're in your pocket.
Where on earth are my gloves? / The dog's gone off with them.
Where on earth are my gloves? / They're on the hall table.
Where on earth are my gloves? / How should I know?
Where on earth are my gloves? / Where you left them, I wouldn't wonder.

Ask this question quite casually when you are going out, leaving a meeting, leaving a friend's house and so on, to see what other replies you can add to your list.

Unobtrusive speechreading practice involving other people

Do-it-yourself practice is not all solitary. The very fact that you have been observing other people and noticing the flowing patterns of speech encourages you to experiment. Of course continue with regular SAS practice but seek opportunities for spontaneous casual contacts too.

At this stage three things matter:
1. To know the subject in advance, helping you anticipate what is likely to be said.
2. That the person talking is speaking quite naturally – you will notice how much people vary when they speak.
3. That you aim to respond quickly.

If you are uncertain, at least say something, even if it is 'Don't know' or 'Aunty will be interested' or 'But never in Japan, I think.'

Find opportunities for spontaneous casual contacts.

I live by the seaside. Every Saturday in summer hundreds of visitors arrive and depart by rail. An enterprising speechreader stood outside the station, looking knowledgeable. Many strangers came to him with questions:

'Where's the shopping centre?'
'Which way to the sea front?'
'Where can we get a taxi?'
'Is there a fission chip shop handy?'
('Yes, there is no 'and' visible; it *does* come over as 'fission'.)
And so on.

Many organizations are desperate for volunteers. If you offer to sell flags or take the money at the door at the coffee morning, anticipate (and practise first with your SAS method) what people are likely to say to you:

'How much are the tickets?'
'Does that include coffee?'
'I haven't any change.'
'Can you change a fiver?'
'When's the draw going to be?'
'What's it in aid of?'
And so on.

Another plan is to ask a question to which you already know the answer. For example, you might approach someone in the bus queue: 'Excuse me, has the Seaford bus gone?' The reply may be a brief yes or no, or something like: 'I hope not, I've been waiting ten minutes' or 'You've just missed it' or 'It was full up but there's a relief behind' or (a nice bonus this) 'It's always late. I'm fed up with this rotten service, no one bothers these days, that's what it is, no one bothers.'

You may decide to ask a passer-by the way to the post office (you know it already actually); then be prepared for: 'First right, opposite the pub.'

'I don't know. I'm a stranger here.'

'The general's by the railway station. It's a long walk.'

'Oh, you want the post office, do you. Well, they sell stamps at the little shop round the corner if it's stamps you're wanting.'

A word of warning! One day I was happily engaged on this useful exercise and got the unexpected reply, 'Good heavens, don't you know where the post office is after living here for fifteen years?' Yes, I just hadn't recognized my next-door neighbour but one ...

Spontaneous conversation often breaks out if you push a pram or own a dog; a cheery 'Good morning' may start things off, and the weather is a topic which you will be familiar with from your SAS mirror practice. You are bound to have added it to your everyday sayings.

What people say depends on their point of view

Circumstances provide clues to likely comments, as do the interests of the speaker. Imagine there is a tree in a field. Different people will view it differently; if the following people see it – the schoolboy, the artist, the bird-watcher, the timber merchant, the farmer, the town planner – which one is likely to want to cut it down because it is in the way? to climb it? to paint it?

Mrs Brown lives at No. 3. The neighbour on the right says, 'Mrs Brown is a real busybody. Old nosy parker's got her finger in every pie, ought to mind her own business.' The neighbour on the left says, 'Mrs Brown is so interested in everyone, I don't know how she makes the time. She cooks the lunch for poor old Alf and looks after the Joneses' dog while they are away and sees to their tomatoes too.'

SAS drill concentrated on rhythm

Now to return to your solitary SAS practice which you have been persisting with so faithfully. This time, notice particularly the rhythm emphasis and pauses. Familiar rhymes are useful because you know them so well. Back to your triple mirror while you say aloud:

> My mother told me
> I never should
> Play with the gypsies
> In the wood.

or   Hot cross buns, hot cross buns,
One a penny, two a penny,
Hot cross buns.

or   Red sky at night shepherd's delight,
Red sky in the morning
Shepherd's warning.

or   You owe me three farthings
Said the bells of St Martin's.

The object is to help you to connect the already familiar sound and sensation of speech, particularly noticing rhythm.

Say the two following sentences (at normal speed of course) whilst feeling the slight pressure as your lips touch:

'My bike was picked up on Monday. The police haven't been able to find it yet.' Your lips meet no less than eight times; you couldn't have said the sentence otherwise.

Here is another sentence:

'Have another helping of plum pudding: It's much better for you than mince pies; no pastry to worry about if you're slimming.' They met nine times in that sentence. (Did you notice that only one sound was used to end 'plum' and begin 'pudding'?)

As you continue with your self-help practice (at normal speed), the three strands of SAS will gradually help you to feel and see sounds subconsciously as they form the living, moving patterns of speech, your own speech and that of other people.

Choice of practice partner (PP)

Ideally it would be splendid if you could find four or five friends who would become practice partners and each spend twenty minutes twice a week doing it *in the right way*. However, this is to expect Utopia. To find even one person is treasure enough. Such people, like rare diamonds, must be carefully chosen. Do not be despondent if it takes time to find one. The wrong kind of 'help' can be an utter disaster and even destroy your ability to speechread.

This is no criticism of people who want to be helpful but is conviction born of sad experience. The wrong 'assistance' can be worse than useless, particularly in the early days when you are forming new habits.

If people think that their speech is being scrutinized, they may feel self-conscious and start to talk in an unnatural way. They may nod their head continuously, exaggerate their speech, speak one word at a time, wave their arms about, keep moving their head from side to side, slow down, mouth words and even speak silently (therefore unnaturally.) This defeats the objective which is for you to follow *ordinary speech.*

It is so good of them to try, they may feel hurt if there is criticism of their efforts, so please take your time and select carefully.

A helpful child may be the answer. They usually speak in a straightforward way; you can tell them what to do without causing resentment; they may be happy to play games like 'I spy', providing natural practice material.

If there is no helpful child handy, it might be worth approaching a local school, for many schools have community service in their programme, a possible source of supply. You might offer to become an aunty or uncle at a children's home. You could greatly enjoy befriending a child, and the school or organization could benefit by children and staff learning more about hearing loss, just through your contact with them.

Assuming that you have found an ideal practice partner, how can you work together? (Hints for practice partners are at the end of this chapter, but the treasure you have found will be eager to read the whole book anyway.)

Preparation for work with PP

A notebook to record what you discover every day, the everyday sayings you meet – the time you give to practice and what you do with it.

A jotting-pad: PP may jot down a thought or two if you both get stuck. Whatever is written is then said again in an ordinary, unexaggerated sentence.

Practice sessions should never be too earnest, too intense or too long. Plan to meet ten minutes before you start in order to have time to greet each other; perhaps snatch a quick cup of tea, put out the cat, check the lighting position and settle down comfortably. Rush, fuss and hustle are not conducive to the alert, calm attention needed from you both.

Self-preparation for PP

You are special because you have been invited to co-operate in a particular way. Your commitment demands at least three things:

Reliability. Don't take on lightly something you may not be able to fulfil. Make a regular arrangement for a definite period of time and then stick to it, come wind or high water. You might decide on half-an-hour's practice period at two definite times each week for the period of one month (never for longer). If something else crops up and it is inconvenient, bad luck. You are committed; someone else will have to deal with the plumber, meet the children or take the dog to the vet. Few things are more disheartening than preparing for a session and, having established a routine, then having it changed.

Dare I say it? Do I know you well enough? To pop in haphazardly for a practice session when it happens to be convenient to you is just not on. Pop in for a chat by all means, but this is not a substitute for the regular routine practice.

Sensitivity. A practice partner would not presume to give advice but is happy to be used to provide whatever type of assistance is needed by the speechreader. Happy is a key word – you should both enjoy working together and find the shared adventure a pleasure. If you are going to become bored or impatient, don't start; do something that you like doing instead.

Be prepared to be guided by the speechreader. You will quickly realize that some days will be better than others.

You will be aware when the speechreader needs a rest. It is a good plan to have a 'five-minute rule': stop after five minutes for a break and a breather before starting again. Never go on too long. Even with the five-minute break, a twenty-minute period is long enough. Half an hour is maximum.

Flexibility. Change to a less demanding exercise if need be. People are at different stages of progress so there is no set material suitable for everyone. General principles are the foundation which different people will build on differently, increasing skill until it becomes second nature and subconscious.

The aim is to understand and respond to whole sentences. The three exercises on page 59 are to encourage subconscious recognition of a known pattern. Use the exact form suggested. Many similar exercises will suggest themselves, always following the same format.

The whole sentence as a unit of understanding. Use short, logical sentences at normal speed, framed in such a way that the reply reveals if it has been understood. If not understood, jot it down for the speechreader and then repeat immediately at normal speed. Always speak *naturally* in ordinary short, logical sentences, at first with a slight pause between sentences. Avoid stilted, artificial material. Use ordinary colloquial English but not obscure language, i.e., don't say 'I've put Maude into the stable' when you mean 'I've put the car into the garage.'

When conversing, be sure the subject is known in advance, stick to the point, be logical. Never repeat one isolated word. If the speechreader's reply indicates that you are not understood, then rephrase the sentence or jot it down so that it can be read and immediately repeat the whole sentence.

I am sure you already articulate well or you would not have been chosen! But guard against exaggerated or unnatural speech. This destroys the rhythmic pattern of the sentence and also destroys progress. Speak clearly, with crisp consonants. Always use your voice but speak very quietly for practice purposes.

Speechreading is demanding. Stick to your rule of a break after five minutes. Do not exceed the set time.

Now a rather advanced point. As you read this book, you will discover that some sounds are easier to see than others. It is a help to know which is which so that you can use visible sounds for preference

– for example, watch yourself saying 'Nice day, isn't it?', and you will agree that not much shows. However, 'What beautiful weather we're having' means the same thing but there are visible clues. On the whole, sentences with long words in them are easier than sentences with short words.

Finally, bear in mind that communication is a shared activity, never competitive, always co-operative. No one is trying to buy or sell or prove anything, but you are, together, enjoying ways towards better communication through speechreading.

Above all be natural, talk normally (although quietly) and enjoy the sessions.

Exercises with PP

Never go on for longer than five minutes without a pause – use a timer so that you pause before you are tired. Prepare in your SAS practice, your time of learning-by-doing.

The two exercises that follow take a long time to describe but are quick and easy to do.

1. Think of the days of the week – there are only seven of them and they all have different sound/appearance/sensation as you say them. As usual you will put them into up-to-time sentences such as:

It's early closing on Wednesday.
I'm going away on Saturday for the weekend.
The Tuesday Club meets at 2.30 on Tuesdays.
Raining as usual – Monday's washing day.
On Thursday I'm having coffee with Mary.
The fish and chip shop opens on Friday at five.

Enjoy the rhythm of the old verse which begins: 'Monday's child is fair of face ...'

You will have noticed that two days of the week are similar in appearance but not exactly the same.

Now comes the time when you meet your practice partner. Throughout, PP will know by your reply if the sentence has been understood correctly. If not, PP will write it down and, after you have read it, repeat the sentence again at normal speed.

Stage A. PP: 'What's the day after ...' (names one day). PP always uses the same format; it is only the day of the week at the end of the sentence that varies. You reply as quickly as possible. This continues at speed, using different days.

Stage B. Same procedure but PP changes format to: 'What's the day after/before ...' (names one day). You reply.

Stage C. PP may use one (or two) day(s) before or one (or two) day(s) after ... and names one day. You will need that break after five minutes.

2. In your preparation SAS practice, use sentences involving numbers, for example:

Never been twenty-one before.

Sweet sixteen and never been kissed.

You're one in a thousand.

I've got a fifty-fifty chance.

Are you all at sixes and sevens?

Every cat has nine lives, some have nine tails.

The four points of the compass.

Two's company, three's none.

The soldiers formed fours in the square.

I want a five-star hotel.

And so on.

The ordinary multiplication tables have good rhythm and go with a swing. You know them and therefore can concentrate on SAS.

By now you will have noticed the numbers which look similar, although they may sound different.

When your practice partner arrives, try the following exercise using only numbers up to twenty-one.

PP uses a prepared list of ten sentences and always begins in the same way: '*Can you tell me how much* are seven and eleven?' You tot up mentally and reply 'Eighteen'. After ten sentences using different numbers, stop and take breath; check which were right. Repeat now that you have read the numbers. Numbers are used for prices, ages, telling the time, dates and so on.

PP always uses an agreed beginning; it is only the ending which changes. For example:

PP: 'Can you tell me half an hour after ...'

(You reply quickly in each case.)

PP always uses an entire sentence up to time, never a number in isolation.

After giving you due warning, the PP then changes to either 'before' or 'after', or uses the twenty-four-hour clock, or the different form of 'quarter to, twenty to, thirteen minutes past' and so on.

The following exercise with your PP requires a number of small objects.

PP puts four of them on the table and then picks up and describes each one, using exactly the same form of sentence. Supposing the four objects were an ash-tray, a teaspoon, a ballpoint pen and a travelling clock, PP would pick up the ash-tray:

The ash-tray is a bluish green colour.

The ash-tray is a blueish green colour.

The ash-tray is about three inches square.

The ash-tray came from Woolworths.

PP describes each object using the same order, starting with the object, and in four sentences says what it is made of, its colour, its size and shape, where it came from. So far you have not responded, but, after all four objects have been described, have a question-and-answer session, always using the same format.

'*What's the ash-tray made of?*'

Reply: '*The ash-tray's made of glass.*'

'*What's the colour of the pen?*'

Reply: '*The pen's yellow.*'

'Where did the travelling clock come from?'

And so on.

You both respond quickly; you both name the object when you reply.

At the next stage the questions leave out the name of the object – for example, 'Which one is round, seven inches long and green?'

You can ask the questions alternately, and there are a lot of them. Always start, 'Which one'. If there is a wrong answer, the speaker picks up the object and repeats the question – now you have a clue and will get it right.

You will certainly need a pause before selecting four more objects. When exactly the same form of sentence is used each time at normal speed, you are not giving your conscious attention to the familiar part of the sentence, but you are doing something even more important – you are absorbing it subconsciously. Your solitary practice on SAS is standing you in good stead.

It is wise to divide your time with PP into two parts. First the structured part (as in the exercises already described) and secondly conversation on a set subject. This also needs preparation.

First choose the subject. Make headings of four different aspects – jot down possible comment for each aspect beforehand. Practise beforehand with SAS so that you are well prepared.

If the subject is a wedding, you might have four headings:

1. *What the bride looked like.* What is likely – Dress? White? Long train? Carrying? Bunch of yellow roses? Veil? Beautiful old Brussels lace? Pretty as a picture?

2. *Best man, bridesmaids, family etc.* What is likely – Three little bridesmaids? Adorable, wearing yellow? Best man was bridegroom's brother? Bride's mother being brave? Large flowered hat?

3. *The service.* What is likely – Music chosen? What the vicar said? Floral decorations? Bells as they left the church?

4. *Reception.* What is likely – Who was there? What they wore? What did they have to eat and drink? Where was it held? What time the happy couple left?

Then you met your PP. The subject is known; the headings are known (particularly necessary in the early stages). The PP talks about the event using the four headings. PP speaks normally but with a small pause between sentences. When PP has finished, describe what you gather the wedding was like. Do not repeat word for word but give the general impression.

If your description is very different from your PP's description, then discuss the four headings together with the 'likely' list you have prepared, and run through the PP's version again. At the end of the session PP talks about the wedding again, telling you all about it, probably in different words (using ordinary, colloquial speech – this time without inserting artificial pauses between sentences). You get the gist of the message and rightly pat yourself on the back.

6. Discoveries about Consonants

Recap

You have discovered some underlying principles to help in following normal everyday speech.

1. People express themselves in many ways. Circumstances, observation and eye contact provide significant clues.

2. People talk in sounds, not in individual words. The natural rhythm of the whole sentence aids understanding. Within it some words may disappear or be squashed together and combine.

3. Your 'language sense' and your lifetime experience of speech assist you to grasp the meaning.

4. In learning-by-doing you use the threefold link of:

Sound	(or memory of sound) of whole sentence	
Appearance	seeing what the sentence looks like	SAS
Sensation	the feeling as you speak	

The following chapter is, in a sense, an optional extra. Some natural speechreaders have acquired skill as you are beginning to acquire it, partly as a subconscious process, certainly not as an intellectual exercise.

One exercise – nine consonants

You have already discovered much through learning-by-doing. Now build on this foundation to find out which of the flexible, moving, flowing sounds of speech can be spotted. An individual sound is a very fleeting part of the whole sentence. You will recall that a sound unnaturally isolated from normal speech is changed, no longer part of the rhythmic pattern and timing of the whole.

SAS practice has revealed that some sounds are associated with a definite appearance/sensation as you say them in sentences.

The following exercise sorts out nine of them.

Here are three people

Bobby Brown aged 7	John Jones aged 54	Winnie Williams aged 35
with fair, curly hair and blue eyes	going a bit thin on top, has brown eyes	with dark, wavy hair and hazel eyes

Let us go through their day and find out what they are doing.

At. 7.30 in the morning

Bobby Brown is eating porridge, brown bread and marmalade.	John Jones is running for a train at the railway station.	Winnie Williams hasn't woken up.

At 11 in the morning

Bobby Brown is in the playground with his bike.	John Jones is chairman at a shareholders' meeting, reading a message. (His secretary's a treasure.)	Winnie Williams is waiting to pay the water rates.

At 1 o'clock

Bobby Brown is having pork and beans, followed by roly-poly pudding	John Jones is having a ham sandwich and an indigestion pill	Winnie Williams is having a cup of weak tea and a Bakewell tart.

At 7.30 p.m.

Bobby Brown is glued to the 'gogglebox'.	John Jones is in his armchair, asleep in front of the telly.	Winnie Williams is at a whist drive.

Use this exercise in do-it-yourself practice. Describe Bobby Brown aloud, and what he is doing at different times of the day, whilst you watch in your mirror connecting sound/appearance/sensation (SAS).

Then do the same with John Jones and Winnie Williams. Be sure to include the name every time. For example you will say.

Winnie Williams is thirty-five.

Winnie Williams has dark, wavy hair and hazel eyes.

At 7.30 in the morning Winnie Williams hasn't woken up.

At 7.30 in the morning Bobby Brown ...

And so on.

Have you noticed that, when talking about Winnie and her doings, you are reminded of the sentences A and B in the last chapter? Look them up and say them again noticing the SAS in your mirror.

It was that same sound which came in each group of sentences A and B (except for one sentence in each group). Did you spot which sentence did *not* include this sound? Repeat the information about Winnie, then repeat the sentence groups A and B. Take your time to work this out, and remember to say the set sentences aloud at normal speed as you see and feel the whole pattern.

Did you spot what was familiar? Yes! The lips puckered and were rather rounded every time a particular sound was made. The particular sound is seen three times in '*W*innie *W*illiams is at the *W*hist drive.'

What do you discover through the sentences about Bobby Brown? Notice that your lips meet often in saying the sentences about him (stick to the exact sentences given, of course) as you SAS.

As you say that *B*obby *B*rown is eating his *P*orridge, *B*rown *B*read and *M*armalade, your lips meet and part seven times. That is another discovery established.

Now what about John Jones? Not so obvious this! And yet the sound which you see when *J*ohn *J*ones is having a ham sandwi*CH* and an indi*G*estion pill also occurs as he runs for a train at the railway sta*SH*un or takes a messa*J* from his secretary (who is such a trea*ZH*ure).

Say all the sentences about John Jones again, and you will see and feel what I mean.

Say the sentences about these three people again (up to normal speed of course), this time going across instead of downwards. Like this:

At 11 a.m. Bobby Brown is in the playground with his bike.	John Jones is chairman at a shareholders' meeting, reading a message. (His secretary's a treasure.)	Winnie Williams is waiting in the queue to pay the water rate.

Notice the rhythm of the whole sentence. Notice the fleeting movement that shows the actual *sound* being made as you speak.

Suggestions with a practice partner

If you have a practice partner, there are three stages of using this exercise that you now know so well.

1. Practice partner asks questions which always include the name of the person. For example:

   What is John Jones doing at 7.30 in the morning?

   What is Winnie Williams doing at one o'clock?

   What is Bobby Brown doing at eleven o'clock in the morning?

And so on.

   You of course, reply immediately.

2. Short sentences, including the name of one of our three friends but differently worded. For example:

   What time is John Jones' shareholder's meeting?

   What does Bobby Brown have for breakfast?

   How old is Winnie Williams?

3. Short sentences without mentioning the name of the person. For example:

   Can you tell me who is going thin on top?

   Can you tell me who is seven years old?

   Can you tell me who has fair, curly hair?

   Can you tell me who is running for a train at the railway station at 7.30 in the morning?

   You will notice that the same format of 'Can you tell me who' is used every time. Why? Yet one more opportunity for you to absorb the general pattern of that group of words subconsciously.

Consonants defined

You have made the discovery that some sounds are easier to see than others. Consonant sounds are the most important sounds in order to understand speech.

How is a consonant different from other sounds made when people talk? Because the flow of breath which comes out of the speaker's mouth meets with a small, brief barrier to its outward flow. This barrier forms the consonant sound. The barrier may be felt in different places. See Chapter 7, 'Speech and Speechreading'.

Remember Bobby Brown with his porridge, bread and marmalade? There the consonant is created and makes the sound when the lips close. It is only momentary, but during that time the flow of the breath out of the mouth is stopped. The way in which the breath escapes after it has been stopped makes the different sort of sound. If the breath escapes through the nose, then it sounds like marmalade – not parmalade or barmalade. If it escapes with a little explosion, it will sound like porridge, not like morridge or borridge. If the vocal cords vibrate, it will become Bobby Brown not Pobby Prown. What matters is the fact that lips are bound to close in order that the flow of breath is stopped, thus forming a consonant sound.

There is a golden rule for speakers and speechreaders: look after the consonants, and the vowels look after themselves. Consonants make sound sense.

The following sentence gives only vowel sounds: '..ea. ..ee.. .e.. ...ou...' It will not make sense, however large it is printed or, if changed into sounds, however loudly it is heard. Yet the same sentence giving only the consonants is understandable, even if the print is small, or if it is heard quietly: 'Cl..r sp..ch g.ts thr..gh.'

Because of the obvious importance of the consonants, the following charts show which are mostly easily seen and which are more difficult to see.

As you look at them, remember that speech is never static but is a flowing pattern of sound. Think of the charts phonetically, not the letters of the alphabet but the actual sounds you hear, see and feel when speaking.

Chart 1   *Consonants fairly easy to see*

Sound	What can be seen/felt	Comment
P, B, M	Lips close	Even the worst speakers close their lips. Try to say 'More beans, please' without closing your lips and you will prove the point
F, V	Lower lip to top teeth	As in 'Very few have fish on Fridays'
TH	Tip of tongue between the teeth	As in 'Thank them on Thursday'
SH, CH J, ZH	Forward lips	As in 'She has a chip on her shoulder.' 'Measure the sugar for the jam'

Chart 2   *Consonants more difficult to see*

S, Z	Breath hisses through almost closed teeth	As in 'The scissors are missing,' 'The centre is busy'
R	Tongue up behind top teeth. Picture varies with different people	As in 'The mirror reflects the roses'
L	Tip of tongue behind top teeth back of tongue maybe visible	As in 'A large parcel from London'
T, D, N	Tongue presses on the gums behind the top teeth	As in 'There's nothing new in today's sale, you know'
K, G, NG	Back of tongue meets junction of hard and soft palate. Tip of tongue behind bottom teeth	As in 'Call the cat. I'm going to lock up.' NG may provide a clue because of the time factor. Compare '*Ring* the bell' and 'Rin*ging* the bell'

Some sounds are 'voiced'; some are not. When 'voiced', there is vibration in the vocal cords, but this does not alter what the sound looks like. (See Chapter 7, 'Speech and Speechreading'.)

How does theory work out in practice?

Because people speak differently, it is unwise to 'lay down the law' about what should be visible. All you can be sure of is that, when people talk, some movements will be made.

As with reading strange handwriting, it can take time to interpret the particular squiggles into sense. The fact that you were taught script at school does not mean that everyone will write to you in script – far from it! You have to decipher many variations in writing to make sense of what is seen. Sometimes it is impossible.

Speechreaders may need to adjust their sights before interpreting an unfamiliar speaker.

However, when a consonant sound is produced, it will have to be formed somewhere by the breath being stopped at some point in order to make the sound. Some consonants, as in '*B*obby's *p*orridge, *b*read *m*armalade for *b*reakfast', are easier to see than others.

Further study of Chart 1

Look again at Chart 1 and you will discover that you already know well over fifty per cent of the sounds, simply because you have been talking so much about Bobby, John and Winnie and their daily doings.

To complete your study of Chart 1, what is SAS when you say:

'Thanks for the birthday present./Just what I wanted.'

'Thelma just never thinks./Thick as two short planks.'

'The thaw set in on Thursday.'

Unfortunately many people seem to lead reasonably contented lives without using the sound of TH at all. 'I haven't seen you for muns and muns,' they say. However, it is still worTH knowng THat, wiTH luck, it may be THere.

If the sound is seen at all, that's a bonus: it's very small at the best of times, although distinctive when present.

The final sound left on Chart 1 is seen in sentences such as:

'*Four fives* are twenty.'
'*Half* a mo, I have to *vote first.*'
'Let's *visit* the a*viary*; it's *full* of *very* beauti*ful* birds.'

Here are a few sentences to start you off, but use any of your learn-by-doing material, being particularly alert to the *sound/appearance/sensation* this time when the lower lip meets top teeth (using normal-speed sentences, of course).

The sink's Filthy, where's the Vim?
I'm Fit as a FiddIe; how are you Feeling?
Friendship is the medicine of liFe.
Free-range eggs are not the same as Farm Fresh eggs.
The Ferry leaves in Five minutes.
A Free-For-all sometimes ends up in Violence.
I'Ve just Fixed my curtains – gold VelVet – they're loVely.
NoVember the FiFth is Guy Fawkes night – let's haVe some Fireworks.

Additional comparison exercises of the last two sounds are in Chapter 8, 'High-Frequency Hearing Loss'.

I suggest that before reading further you go through this chapter again, as part of your learn-by-doing routine work.

Study of Chart 2

Truly a flexible approach is a speechreader's friend!

Say the following piece aloud, as part of your SAS learn-by-doing study:

My grandmother had a squirrel. The squirrel's name was Ermintrude. My grandmother was a remarkable woman; she was a great believer in reincarnation.

She was convinced that the squirrel was the reincarnation of my great-great-grandmother whose name was Ermintrude. That's why the squirrel was called Ermintrude.

You may be one of those people who do not produce the rrrolling 'r' sound. Now imagine this being said by someone with slightly protruding front teeth who doesn't produce the sound of 'rrr' or 'th' at all. It might sound (and therefore look and feel) like:

My Gwandmuver had a squiwwel. The squiwwel's name was

Ermintwude. My gwandmuver was a wemarkable woman; she was a gwate believer in weincarnation.

She was convinced that the squiwwel was the weincarnation of my gweat-gweat-gwandmuver, whose name was Ermintwude. That's why the squiwwel was called Ermintwude.

Once you were used to the general pattern of the speaker's delivery, you would quickly make sense of what was said.

You will have noticed from Chart 2 that the actual sound made when people talk about 'round robins' or 'red herrings' or 'reading', 'writing' and 'arithmetic' may vary (although not always as dramatically as in the squirrel story). It so happens that my own front teeth protrude slightly, and other people, until they are used to the way I talk, sometimes might think I have said 'chest of draws' instead of 'Rest, of course'. When I say, 'John Jones is running for his train', it looks not unlike, 'Ron Rhodes is shunning for his train.' It is the sound you SAS.

Sentences for comparison

It is useful to compare sounds which are similar, although not exactly the same, as in the following pairs of sentences. Sometimes the pairs of sentences are themselves similar because they share the same rhythmic pattern.

These sentences *should not be used* with a practice partner but are designed for you to make discoveries during your SAS do-it-yourself practice.

1. The *rent* was due in September.
2. She *went* out in a temper.

1. Poor little *rich* girl.
2. Do you take '*Which*' magazine?

1. *Rose* trees enjoy a shower of rain.
2. *Woe's* me! I'm late again.

2. Are you taking me for a *ride*?
2. Which soap powder washes *white*?

Some speakers and some accents include more of the RRR sound than others.

In the south of the UK the final RRR is not usually sounded at all, but a final RRR may appear unexpectedly in such sentences as 'War

Ron Want' and 'Westminster Rabbey is very old.'

Now a different sound from Chart 2. Please look in your mirror and sing a tune. Any tune will do, no words, just la-la-la-la-la. Splendid. Once more. This time watch your tongue.

Busy isn't it! You can *see* the back of your tongue, *feel* its pressure behind your top teeth and also observe its flashing downward movement. Now watch again. 'Well, that's easy, anyway,' you think. But not quite so easy when the mouth is in a less open position. You can see this sound without much effort in the following examples:

'*L*augh and the world *l*aughs with you.'

'She dropped the *l*ighted oi*l l*amp and gave a *l*oud scream.'

But it's not so obvious in this context: 'I'm hoping to *l*ive in *L*ondon, it's a *l*ittle nearer home. As usua*l* there's nothing to *l*et, the agents just won't *l*isten un*l*ess you want to se*ll*.'

Now watch for the picture made by this sound in everyday conversation:

'He*ll*o! Would you *l*ike a *l*ift? I'm going to the *l*ibrary.'

'I've *l*ost my wa*ll*et, I be*l*ieve I *l*eft it on the ta*bl*e over there – sha*ll* I te*ll* the po*l*ice?'

'Isn't the *l*aburnum *l*ove*l*y! A*ll* those c*l*usters of ye*ll*ow b*l*ossom … do the f*l*owers sme*ll* at a*ll*?'

Remember my remarks about words running into each other? Did you notice that 'table over' *sounds* and therefore looks like 'tay-blover'?

Compare this sound with another old friend which may look similar but which is not actually the same.

1. What do you know about your *r*ights?
2. What do you know about ancient *l*ights?

1. Two *w*rongs don't make a right.
2. It's too *l*ong since *l*ast we met.

1. It still pours with *rain* every day.
2. The right-hand *lane* goes to the motorway.

1. My *wrist* aches. I hope it's not sprained.
2. My *list* is ready. I hope it's not too lengthy.

Before proceeding further with Chart 2, let us stop for a practical exercise, a reminder that the objective of speechreading is to understand the message. To continue with the theoretical work for too long can prevent progress; it should be only a supplement to your SAS practice. Therefore the following exercise is deliberately inserted here.

Practical interlude

Your equipment is one other person and a lot of unfussy, full-page coloured pictures, grouped into subjects (for example, fashion models, house interiors, different types of buildings). Glossy magazines, large calendars and catalogues are good sources of supply.

Sit opposite your partner who has not seen the pictures. Allow your partner to see one picture for about three seconds only. Ask questions about it, one question per sentence. For example:

How many people in the picture?
What is the woman holding in her hand?
How many windows are there?
What colour is the front door?
And so on.

Partner replies to each question immediately, by a whole sentence. For example, the reply to the last question must not be 'yellow' (one word) but 'The house has a yellow front door' (whole sentence).

If the answers are not accurate, never mind. At the end of all the questions, show your partner the picture again for a long look before going on to another picture.

The next stage is when you both have a set of pictures (not previously seen by the other person). Take it in turns to show a picture and ask questions. The answers to your own questions are easy because there is a limited range of probable replies.

Asking and answering questions

The snag about questions is that they often come out of the blue, with no context to help you. Sometimes a question may be implied by tone of voice (which is invisible, of course) or may be asked in a roundabout, ambiguous way.

In a direct question, it may be the very first group of words that reveal that a question is being asked. These groups of words can be noticed and woven into your SAS practice, using each form several times but with a different ending, thus:

Which way to the post office?
Which way to the swimming-pool?
Which way to the police station?

Which would you rather have, brown or white bread?
Which would you rather have, tea or coffee?
Which would you rather have, butter or marge?
When shall we meet again?
When shall we have supper?
When shall we collect the children from school?
Will you be at home this evening?
Will you be coming back for lunch?
Will you be going to the supermarket?

Always say the whole sentence up-to-time, using the same form several times with different endings.

You will notice that in the above examples the helpful puckered lips give a clue; therefore make these your first practice target. Use the same form several times with a different ending. Some practice material could be:

What are you doing at nightschool?
What are you doing with that shotgun?
Why are you asking so many questions?
Why are you so inquisitive?
Where shall I find a ... ?
Would you mind if ... ?
What did she say about ... ?
What do you think about ... ?

Make up at least three
different endings.
Say the whole sentence.

Go on to explore the fund of other direct question forms in the same way. They will not all have that helpful lip pucker. For example:

Can you meet me at ... ? (several different endings)
Can you tell me why ... ?
Could you please ... ?
Would you mind ... ?
Did you go to ... ?
Have you ever met ...?

Sometimes only one word indicates the question:

What's the time?
What's all the fuss about?

What's the problem?
Who's in charge?
Who's that?
Who's left their glasses behind?
How's aunty?
How's the time?
even How's that?

This brings me to questions which do not require a reply – often these are statements or rhetorical questions:

Who does she think she is anyway?
What a waste of time!
What utter nonsense!
Why don't you mind your own business?
What couldn't I do with a cuppa!
Did you ever see the like!
Who cares! Who knows! What a shame!
Why doesn't she look where she's going?
What weather!
Why worry! Why not!

As if that were not enough, there are also questions put in an ambiguous way:

I don't know whether you've any information about ...
I really don't like to bother you, but could you possibly tell me ...

and questions that are implied rather than stated:

I believe you collect Staffordshire ware (do you?)
You've probably never met Mrs Jones (have you?)
You will have another slice (won't you?)
I wonder if you can come on Monday (can you?)
I doubt if you'll make it tonight (will you?)

(See also Chapter 11, 'Listening Tactics and Social Strategy', for the closed or open question technique.)

Consonant charts continued

Having enjoyed this practical interlude, back to the nitty-gritty, we return to Chart 2. There are only three more groups of sounds left to study.

When you say, 'The scissors are missing' or 'The Centre is busy, absolutely buzzing with activity', what do you notice?

This sound cannot be made unless the teeth are close together for the breath to hiss through. (If you need proof, repeat the two sentences again and see what happens if your teeth are not close together.) Say the same sentences normally, and you will see and feel the particular movement that creates the slight hiss as the sound is made. Notice this sound as you say aloud the following sentences:

People feel *listless* after 'flu.
I wish you *success* in your exam.
When does the off-*licence* open?
Did you get the *message*?
Ea*sy* come, ea*sy* go.

In the second of the following pairs of sentences, the indicated word is preceded by the slight hiss we are studying. Say each pair of sentences several times at normal speed to spot the slight difference:

1. She means no *harm*.
2. They sang a *psalm*.

1. The *oar* is in the boat.
2. The *saw* is in the shed.

1. The crinoline is a dress with a *hoop*.
2. The saucepan is full of vegetable *soup*.

1. You're always up bright and *early*.
2. He's always abrupt and *surly*.

1. Have something to *eat*.
2. Won't you take a *seat*?

We have now studied three groups of consonants from the five groups in Chart 2. These three sounds are often combined with other consonants. The repetition of pairs of sentences for comparison helps you to build *subconscious recognition*.

Compare the '*Winnie Williams* pucker' when it is preceded by the slight hiss of 'sss'. Do you notice any difference?

1. Have you made your *will*?
2. Fling the potatoes into the pig *swill*.

1. *Weep* no more, lady.
2. *Sweep* the dust under the carpet.

1. Cross your fingers and *wish*.
2. *Swish* the duster over the car windows.

In the following sentences it is the sound as in '*L*augh and the world laughs with you' which is combined with the small hiss of sss in the second sentence of the pair.

1. *Light* the gas. Where are the matches?
2. *Sleight* of hand? Yes, he's a magician.

1. Can you *leap* over the wall?
2. Can you *sleep* through it all?

1. You're *late* again – what's the excuse?
2. A *slate* fell off the roof.

We must press on ('slater than you think) to compare the closed lips of 'Bobby's porridge, bread and marmalade for breakfast', when preceded by the small hiss of sss.

1. Put that in the *pending* tray.
2. I'm *spending* every penny on my holiday.

1. A William *pear* has a special flavour.
2. Can the *spare* parts be replaced easily?

1. The travelling expenses are *paid* in advance.
2. Fetch your bucket and *spade*, we're going to the seaside.

(Did you notice this sound in 'ek*s*pen*s*es?)

1. Legend and *myth* are woven into history.
2. The black*smith* works in the old forge.

It is interesting that when this sound is used with vibration of vocal cords, this changes a *bus* into a *buzz, fussy* into *fuzzy, sink* into *zink* and so on, but the appearance – what you see – remains unaltered.

Only two groups of consonants remain to be tackled. However, having studied all the other consonants as they are spoken in ordinary rhythmic sentences, you may have used these two groups so often that you have been assimilating them automatically. In the T.D.N. group, it is easy to be aware of the feeling of the tongue pressing behind the top teeth as you speak. Feel and see the sounds as you say aloud:

Tut tut tut – how you do surprise me!
Dear, dear, dear, some people do mutter.
No, no, no, never, but never, again.
Hold the ladder so it won't wobble.
Come to dinner on Saturday or Sunday.
Do you play table tennis or ping-pong?
What's the matter? Post my letter.
Feeling better? Have a natter.
Finda baby sitter. Drinka pinta.

The K.G.NG consonants are almost invisible so I have left them until last. Remember that the sound is not like the spelling. The 'K' sound happens in sentences like:

Koncentrate on the Kontext.

Katie was kross and so she kicked the kat.

What is known as a hard G sound happens in sentences like: 'Give me some bubble-gum.' It looks the same as the sound of 'K'. The soft G is really a J, as you will see when you say, 'Just like Jeorge; forgot his jymshoes again,' and so is part of a group in Chart 1.

You will remember that a consonant sound is formed when there is some momentary barrier to the flow of breath from the mouth. The barrier is made in different ways. When it is produced by the lips closing, as in 'Bobby's porridge and marmalade for breakfast', then it is very easily seen.

However, the sounds we are studying now are made when the back of the tongue meets the junction of the soft and hard palate; a slight twitch of the double chin may be observed as a barrier is released, allowing the breath to flow. This sound in the NG form does not even provide a twitch, but it can be spotted by the rhythm. Compare 'sing me a song', 'singing me a song', 'have a good laugh', 'having a good laugh'.

One expert speechreader I know finds that polo-neck sweaters and flowing beards make it more difficult for him to speechread the wearer, because that telling little twitch is not visible!

In the following examples you will discover this group of sounds as you say the whole sentence aloud, but you will 'see' them mainly in your imagination, through context and that possible twitch under the chin.

Going, going, gone!

I'm flying to Hong Kong.

They say 'King Kong' is coming to Croydon.

'Cash and Carry' is becoming commonplace.

Fire-crackers go bang, bang, bang.

Come, come, come. Pull yourself together.

Put the kettle on the gas quickly.

I want a cup of strong black coffee.

(By this time I feel sure you want one too.)

To summarize our discoveries so far. Always use sentences said up to time, *never* individual words.

Consonant sounds which look the same
P-B-M   T-D-N   F-V   S-Z   SH-CH-J-ZH   W-WH   K-G-NG
Those which are similar but not the same
L ... T-D-N   W ... R   L ... R
Those which are easy to see
P-B-M   V-F   TH   SH-CH-J-ZH   W-WH
Those which are more difficult to see
S-Z   T-D-N   K-G-NG   R   L

Combinations of consonants

Consonant sounds may combine:

sp	sm	sw	sl	st	sn	sk	
fr	br	pr	tr	cr	gr	dr	tw
fl	bl	pl	cl	gl			

Some of these consonants' combinations have already been shown in sentences.

To absorb the small differences, short sentences for comparison are ideal learn-by-doing SAS material, such as:

1. A *lean* joint of beef.
2. A *clean* sweep's a relief.

1. It's *cold* outside.
2. Don't *scold* the child.

1. Lovely *kippers* for supper.
2. That *skipper's* no land lubber.

Some consonant combinations are not immediately obvious; for example, the sound of 'KS' is seen when people talk about 'e*x*cellent food, but e*x*cessively e*x*pensive'.

The sound of KW occurs if they say:

'She was so *q*uiet, I thought it was rather *q*ueer', 'The ducks waddled along *q*uite *q*uickly going "*q*uack, *q*uack, *q*uack" all the time.'

Homophenes

Before leaving consonant sounds, you will notice that in both charts some of them are grouped together. This is because they look the same.

'Homophenes' are words which look the same when spoken; for example, Pat Bat Mat look identical, and without context there is no knowing which is which. However, if someone says, 'Wipe your feet on the mat,' it is unlikely that you would mistake it for 'Wipe your feet on the Pat' or 'the Bat'.

You may recall that the sounds of T, D, N look the same on the lips too. Therefore Pat Bat Mat might also be Pan Ban Man or even Pad Bad Mad. However, speed speechreaders are busy thinking of the sense of what is being said, of grasping a *total message*, rather than single words.

Miss X had read about homophenes in a book. 'Lip-reading's impossible,' she said despairingly 'P, B and M look the same.' However, she understood perfectly when asked to shut the window, hand round the tea and keep an eye on Mrs Blogging's baby that was a bit restive. It took a long time to convince her that she was already able to speechread in spite of homophenes!

A beginner asked an expert speechreader 'what do you do about homophenes?' The expert looked blank. 'I don't know,' he replied. 'I just speechread what people are saying.'

We are told by those who study the rules of aerodynamics that a bumble bee is entirely the wrong shape to fly. It is a scientific fact that its body is far too big and its wings impossibly small. Luckily no one has told the bumble bee! In blissful ignorance that what it is doing is not possible, it continues to buzz around undeniably airborne. It even has the audacity to fly quite long distances. Let us hope it never finds out about the laws of aerodynamics.

The bumble bee illustrates the reason why I want you to concentrate on understanding the speaker's message in spite of some sounds looking the same.

Throughout this study of consonants, you have ignored the spelling. Always think of the sound; always say the exercise aloud in your learn-by-doing programme.

Finally, three thoughts:

1. Care about the consonants.
2. An example of flexible speechreading. A friend, an excellent speechreader, was at a party. Her husband said to her, 'The thauthageth are on thicth. The black thpoth are thethamy theeth. They're quite thafe.' Yes. He had a slight lisp and always used 'th' instead of 's'!
3. An extract from *Jonathan Livingstone Seagull* by Richard Bach: 'Look with your understanding, find out what you already know, and you'll learn the way to fly.'

7. Speech and Speechreading

The familiarity of speech

Speech and speechreading are like the heavenly twins. They go together. They are closely related.

Speech has been a part of our inner being ever since early childhood. You learned to speak a long time ago and, no doubt, you have talked a good deal since then. Speech patterns are formed at an early age and are firmly established – part of our way of life, an almost subconscious activity, rather in the same way as chewing or walking.

This is why speechreading is no stranger to you. You have been surrounded by speech and using it for most of your life. Your own speech habits, articulation, inflection, intonation, were learnt long ago.

You already possess that invisible asset of 'inner speech' which is a priceless advantage. Have you ever watched people reading to themselves, slow readers who move their lips silently as they read? Their movements reflect their aural memory at work; their own 'inner speech' is helping them to interpret what they read.

Chapter 9, 'Living Language', points out that this aural memory-bank of speech and language continues to grow, and like all growing things it needs nourishing.

Talking (even if it is talking to yourself or your dog or your prize marrow) nourishes and builds your aural memory-bank and uses your own 'speech experience' which aids speechreading. So does reading aloud. So do memorizing and repeating with relish what you have memorized.

In this chapter we are looking a little more closely at speech, the 'twin' of speechreading. You already know and experience speech subconsciously because you have been doing it successfully for years and years and years. It can tell you a lot about speechreading.

The mechanism

This illustration shows the 'speech apparatus' in the form of a diagram.[10]

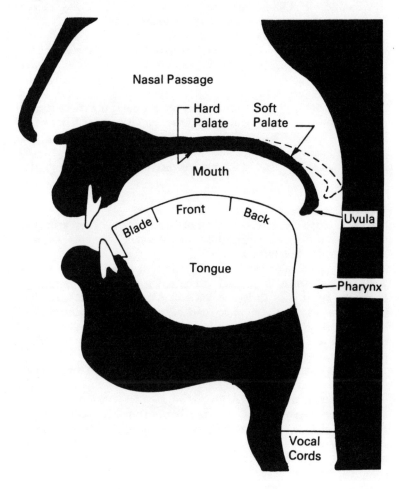

It is the use of this 'apparatus' which enables people to express themselves in speech and which gives speech its quality and pattern. On no account worry about the following technicalities, but, as with driving a car, it is helpful to know what is under the bonnet.

When people talk, air from the lungs is forced through the larynx into the mouth or nose to escape finally into the outside world.

When sounds are said to be 'voiced', they are produced with vibration. This happens when there is a voluntary tightening of the vocal cords which sets vibration in motion as the air is on its journey from the lungs. When sounds are unvoiced, the vocal cords are relaxed to allow the air a completely free passage. No vibration is caused by the vocal cords because they are not being put into action.

You will see from the illustration that the vocal tract has several resonant cavities. These amplify the sound as well as giving it a particular quality. The shape and size of these cavities can be changed by the articulators – that is, the jaw, tongue, teeth, lips and soft palate.

Breath

Singers are usually very easy to speechread. Why? They articulate well and do not run out of breath before the end of a sentence, because they are used to breathing adequately.

Breath is the fundamental necessity.

Good breathing is easy, quiet and deep. On the contrary in shallow breathing, sometimes known as clavicular breathing, quick, shallow breaths are taken into the upper part of the chest. Often this sort of breathing is accompanied by raising the shoulders and pushing forward the front part of the chest; it does not take in much air or provide the opportunity to have much control over it.

You may like to check yourself when you are relaxing on your back on the floor as suggested at the end of Chapter 12.

In order to do this,

1. Place your fingers an inch or two below your breastbone (that is the bone which begins in front of your chest where your neck finishes).

2. Drawn your hands away from each other until the fingers are about six to eight inches apart. Your hands will now be resting lightly over your ribs.

3. Take your deep, quiet, slow breath and feel your ribs expanding sideways as the air fills your lungs. The ribs will move back to their resting-place again as you allow yourself to breathe out.

How different is this deep breathing from the shallow, uncontrolled breathing which uses only a very small part of the lungs. Correct breathing helps to clear the mind and to reduce tension. Naturally it helps speech. The voice is less likely to become a thin, breathless squeak. The sentences are less likely to run out of puff in mid-stream and trail off into inaudibility. The speaker is less likely to gulp for more air in mid-sentence.

Your own speech as a speechreading aid

We have already noticed that speech consists of vowels and consonants and that crisp, clearly articulated consonants are particularly important for the clarity of speech. People who do not articulate well are more difficult to speechread.

You will remember that consonant sounds are made by creating a brief barrier to the flow of breath. It is the organs of articulation which are used to create this barrier. The consonants are grouped together phonetically, depending on the kind of sound they make. The groups are given different names.

'Nasals', for example, is the name given to sounds which are made when the breath escapes through the nose. There are three of them, as in the following sentences:

No, no, it was*n*'t me. I'm *n*ever there on Wed*n*esdays.'

'*M*ary, you're *m*arvellous. What a *m*agnificent *m*emory you've got.'

'The so*ng*s you are si*ng*ing belo*ng* to the Victorian age.'

'A cry that shivered to the ti*ng*li*ng* stars.'

Say these sentences while you rest a finger on the side of your nose, and you will feel the vibration. The vibration cannot be seen, of course. It is not considered friendly to grab the nose of the person speaking with you. In any event, if you are within arm's length, you are too close for optimum speechreading. Remember you need to see the *whole* face and expression, including the eyes of the speaker.

If people have a bad cold, the nasal cavity gets blocked up and so they cannot say the sounds properly. They are likely to substitute another sound. They might say the second of the three sentences as: 'Bary, you're barvellous. What a bagnificent bebory you've got' They are likely to say: 'I'll dever say dough agaid' instead of 'I'll never say no again.' I wonder if you can 'hear' the difference in your mind's ear?

Some groups of consonants *sound* similar and therefore could easily be misheard, they *look* different and *feel* different when you say them. (This is one more reason why SAS practice pays dividends.)

Compare with do-it-yourself SAS:

Is your nylon *nightie* fireproof?
The hurricane was *mighty* fierce.

Will you *mow* the lawn?
Did you *know* the time?

See what I mean? 'Nightie' and 'mighty' may sound alike but they look and feel entirely different, as do 'mow' and 'know', 'mew' and 'new', 'night' and 'might'; compare them in up-to-time sentences.

Conversely, some sounds look similar but *sound* different. Often the only difference depends on whether or not the sound is voiced. Vibration of the vocal cords cannot be seen.

In ordinary flowing speech, the whole sentence happens so quickly that, even if you held the speaker firmly by the throat, it would not be easy to spot vibration of quickly passing consonant sounds. The concentration on detail and the speaker's reaction might prevent you from grasping the speaker's meaning anyway.

Some consonants

Here are some sentences in which two consonant sounds are identical to look at but sound slightly different because one is voiced (the vocal cords vibrate) and the other is unvoiced.

Voiced: 'You're *very* late. What's the reason?'
Unvoiced: 'The *ferry's* late, I suppose they're on strike again.'
Voiced: 'My own *vine* and fig tree.'
Unvoiced: 'I'm *fine*, absolutely in the pink.'

In case anyone wants to have a tidy note of the way consonants are classified, there are many books which will give you details. The sounds are grouped together under different names:

Plosives, Fricatives, Affricates, Nasals, Laterals, Frictionless, Semi-vowel. To be honest, I do not recommend you to study them. You will remember that: 'The speed speechreader wants to know the answer, not how he arrived at it ... he pieces together the sense from a few fragments.'

All consonants are 'voiced' with the exception of p, t, k, s, f, th (as in thin), sh, h, ch.

An example of how little it matters to the speechreader is the sound of TH as in:

Voiced: 'Do you want these or those put there?'
Unvoiced: 'Don't be a thickhead. Think, man, think.'

I cannot give even one example where the meaning is changed in any way if the TH sound is voiced or not. In practice you will probably be lucky if it is seen at all!

The vowels

Although it is the consonant sounds which are essential for understanding speech, I am in duty bound to mention the vowel sounds too.

You have already noticed in your SAS practice of up-to-time sentences that sometimes the mouth seems to open more noticeably than at others. Any different shapes you have noticed in the rapid pattern of flowing speech will vary depending on the speaker, but even so, some shapes will be slightly different from others.

You will remember, too, that vowel sounds are those which come out of the mouth without any barrier to the flow of voiced breath.

In English, the vowels are grouped into

vowels and **SHORT** vowels.

The long ones are stronger and louder and, as you would expect, longer in duration than the short ones, which are very short, very quick and very fleeting.

Compare: 'Take your big *feet* off my best chair' (long vowel) and 'My new shoes don't *fit*. They pinch my big toe' (short vowel).

For speechreaders, the most important are the five long vowels. Here they are:

AH as in yard, aha! Raj, fast, shan't
AW as in awful, ought, oar, awe, ore, tore, cor! caught, war
OO as in cool, rule, blue, rue, pool, school
ER as in worse, early, sir, bird, learn, church, fur
EE as in seize, wheeze, knees, tea, been

These can be thought of as five somewhat different shapes, but it must be remembered that when people are talking they will be rapidly moving shapes.

A rather exaggerated illustration below shows the five long vowels roughly classified:[11]

AH Open mouth	
AW Smaller opening	
OO Mouth like a button	
ER Lips apart	
EE Lips elongated *(like a smile)*	

Say the following short sentence up-to-time using the do-it-yourself SAS method. As you see the rhythm and natural pauses, also notice the slightly different shapes of the five long vowels (in italics).

'*Ah*! There's the donkey. I'll call him. Neddy boy – come, come – *EE-AW, EE-AW*! He's coming. He thinks that I'm a donkey too – *OO – ER*! He tried to kick me.'

In your do-it-yourself practice you can try to spot long vowels by contrasting two of them with each other in sentences. For example AH and EE.

AH: The *army marched past* with *smart* uniform and good discipline.

EE: *Easy* come, *easy* go – we shan't *see* him before the *Easter* holidays.

AH: *Half* a mo – I *shan't* be long.

   Blast! the *car* won't *start*.

   I *can't* move it. *Aren't* you going to push?

   Keep *calm!* Wave your *arms*, use your *charm*.

   Wish I had a horse 'n *cart*.

EE: The cat has *fleas*.

   The child has dirty *knees*.

   I'll never pay the *fees*.

   The lawn is full of *weeds*.

   The beehive has no *bees*.

   Lightning has struck the *tree*.

   I fear I'm going to *sneeze*.

You could then make up some sentences in which AH could be compared with another long vowel, say AW, like this:

   The strong *arm* of the *law*.

   You've dropped the *mar*malade on the *floor*.

   He may be an *artful* dodger but he's never a *bore*.

It is useful to compare differences rather than to look for one shape in isolation. It is useful, too, to choose the most obvious shape (in this case AH) and then contrast the others with it in turn. I would suggest that this is essentially a do-it-yourself exercise and becomes part of your general observation of speech, bearing in mind that different accents and ways of speaking will influence what you see/hear.

For example, in the south of England the word 'bath' will rhyme with art and harp, but in the north a short vowel is more likely – bath, giraffe, path and laugh, will rhyme with hat, fat, sat, cat.

There are six short vowels, as in the following sentence:

That pen is not much good

1   2   3   4   5   6

You will take these in your stride without much ado if you are concentrating on the sense of the sentence, noticing the crisp consonants.

Another sound very common in English speech, *the neutral vowel*, is shown as ∂ there is no letter of the alphabet which corresponds). It is almost like a little grunt and occurs in sentences but not necessarily when one word is spoken on its own – another good reason why you should always speechread the sentence as a unit, not looking for individual words.

The neutral vowel occurs twice in this sentence: 'Let's use the chi*na* teapot *again*.' Always SAS the sounds you are comparing by using short sentences *at normal speed*.

Much of the easy flow of speech depends on the neutral vowel. Vowels move towards a neutral form when used in naturally flowing sentences. In natural conversation the smooth flow and blending of sounds mean that whole phrases make a phonetic whole. Phrases like:

How do you do?   (Howjudo)
Fish and chips   (Fishnchips)
Bacon and eggs   (Baconeggs)

are seen as a whole, and the unity should not be destroyed.

Diphthong

If two vowels combine, they form a diphthong, the two shapes blending into each other in quick succession. With some speakers the difference is not very obvious.

Do-it-yourself practice compares the visible differences in sentences which are spoken naturally at normal speed, but not exaggerated.

Open lips which quickly change to the more elongated shape of the long vowel IE may be seen in two different forms. Compare the shape of diphthong IE as in:

My pork *pie* has gone off.
Would you *like* a *ripe* pear instead?
Do spare *time* to drop me a *line*.

With the diphthong AY, as in:

We meet from *day* to *day*.
My *name* was on the *label*.
I like to *pay* my *way*.

They are similar, but the initial mouth opening is larger in the first group than in the second.

This time combine AH with OO (long vowel no. 3) and they form the sound seen in:

They've a *house* in *town*.
The *crowds* waving flags were *shouting loudly*.
Now is the moment. Don't make a *sound*.

The diphthong OA is the same but with the initial mouth opening being smaller as in:

I *know* there's a window *open*.
I *told* you so! I'll catch a *cold*.

Where's my *coat*? Let's go *home*. I'm chilled to the *bone*.

Having used these twelve sentences in your do-it-yourself practice and been aware of the sound (or memory of sound) and of the slight differences which are visible, you may like to compare two sentences, each from a different group, specially noticing if you can spot any difference in the diphthong shapes.

So far you have thought about four diphthongs (each illustrated by three sentences):

IE as in island, mighty, sigh, kind, tight, fight.

AY as in cave, wave, lake, wakefulness, tame, same, safe.

OW as in mouth, bounce, downwards, noun, foundling, cow, slough.

OA as in old, goat, boat, soak, poke, Oates, voter.

Naturally you will practise such words *only* in up-to-time sentences because seen out of context they are misleading.

You may have noticed that I have not suggested any intensive practice specifically on vowels or their different combinations into diphthongs. Vowels are recognized most effectively as part of the pattern and rhythm of the whole sentence. They are flexible, varying to some extent according to the speaker; there is not the same definite articulation as with consonant sound. With vowels you are relying more on sound (or memory of sound) and on appearance than on the feeling of the movements of your own 'speech organs'.

The next two diphthongs are almost exactly the opposite of each other and therefore less likely to be confused.

The first is seen in:

Pour *oil* on troubled water.
Clay is good *soil* for roses.
Do you prefer champagne or beer with *oysters*?

Combine EE (long vowel no. 5) with OO (long vowel no. 3) and you will have another diphthong, as in:

The *tulips* are in bloom.
Dance in the *dew* on 1st May.
Chew over the idea, it may be *useful*.

Finally the rather nondescript parted lips for the sound of ER (long vowel no. 4) may be preceded by two slightly different sounds, as in

A – ER:
The Norwegians often have *fair hair*.
Wear a muffler in the cold night *air*.
Take *care*! Mind how you go.

E – ER:

Some people have *weird ideas* about speechreading.
Dry your *tears*, we are *here*, never *fear*.
Steer clear of the *weir*, safer to fish from the *pier*.

In a *tripthong* there are three parts. You start with one vowel, go on to another and end with the third. The three sounds combine and blend, and the whole process is very rapid.

Here are some examples:

1. Get out! You're a *liar*.
   Help, help! There's a *fire*!
   She's a real live *wire*.

2. The train went *slower* and *slower*.
   Horse no. 7 is a fast *goer*.
   Show 'er the way, mate.

3. There's another *power* cut.
   Do have a *shower*.
   You're always a *tower* of strength.

I would suggest that the consonants and the context are what you need rather than worrying about small differences that are flexible, depending on the speaker.

Voice and hearing

We all modulate our voice through hearing it. We speak as we hear speech. This pattern is firmly established in very early life.

This is one reason why hearing impairment in childhood is totally different from hearing loss in adult life. A child learns to talk by imitation. A baby with perfect hearing will not learn to talk unless it is with people who talk – and then it will pick up whatever language it hears, which becomes the child's primary language.

When hearing loss of any degree happens in adult life, the speech patterns have already been firmly established, but there are two points worth attention.

Articulation and voice volume

No one, however sharp their hearing, can know what their own voice sounds like from the outside. We can only hear our own voice as it sounds to us when we speak. People who hear themselves for the first time on a tape-recorder often find it hard to believe that the stranger talking is actually them. 'That can't be *me*,' they say – sometimes aghast, sometimes glowing with delighted amazement.

If someone has suffered severe hearing loss for many years and suddenly is able to hear well through an aid, he is likely to have the same experience of surprise.

One advantage of using a hearing-aid is in hearing one's own voice 'from the outside' – the aid microphone picks up the voice of the user as well as voices of other people. An aid can be very helpful in the monitoring of speech and voice and in helping to assess the amount of background noise.

The SAS method of practising speechreading helps to prevent speech articulation becoming slovenly, especially when hearing-aids cannot fully compensate for hearing loss.

Background noise

We modulate our voice depending on the circumstances, particularly in relationship to background noise. Voice volume is automatically monitored by fitting our voice loudness to suit the circumstances and environment.

Imagine the different voice that might be used in: telling a bedtime story to a sleepy six-year-old; chatting with a friend in a quiet sitting-room; giving a speech at a regimental dinner; dealing with a group of bouncing, shouting, enthusiastic teenagers in a bare hall.

If severe or total hearing loss interferes with the in-built automatic 'volume control' of voice, what can be done about it?

Ideally we need a small instrument worn like a wristwatch which would indicate the loudness of background noise. The voice could then be raised until the instrument responded to it above the level of the background noise. Such an instrument is not yet perfected, although work is progressing.

Awareness of environment may give at least some idea if it is quiet or not. Obviously it is likely to be quiet in an empty hall or in a field; it is likely to be noisy when a crowd of people are talking together all at the same time.

Much will depend on acoustics. A small group of people using the public baths can be very noisy indeed. Sounds will be reflected by the shiny tiled walls and also bounce back from the surface of the water.

In other circumstances there may be invisible hazards like piped music in shops and restaurants, juke boxes in pubs or cafés, the rumble of loud traffic passing outside. The noise may be loud enough for you to feel the vibration: the disco seems to hit more than one's ear – the very room vibrates! At cocktail party noise level everyone has to shout simply because everyone is shouting.

Naturally you will watch the person you are talking with to notice if they appear to have difficulty in hearing you because of background noise. It is invaluable to have a friend who can indicate to you by some private sign if you should raise or lower your voice.

Mr B, who had totally lost his hearing, had to read a lesson in York Minster at a national rally of Scouts. One boy, sitting near the front, leant forward slightly if the reader's voice volume needed raising and leant back slightly if it was too loud. By keeping an eye on him, the reader was able to feel confident that he was audible. (How often one wishes that readers who have no hearing loss would take the trouble to follow the same procedure!)

Tone

We have seen from the illustration of the speech apparatus that there are various empty spaces in the system. These act as resonators. They amplify the sound of speech and give it 'body'. Many people do not use these resonators fully, and this may cause their throat to feel strained and their tone of voice to sound thin and forced. For most people (whether or not they have any loss of hearing) it is an advantage to use the resonators fully.

The following exercise would take only a few minutes every day. It consists of three positive steps.

1. Close your lips lightly and hum. When your voice is 'forward', this should make the lips vibrate and cause a tingling sensation. If you do not feel the tingling, repeat the hum but make it lower in pitch. Eventually, when the pitch is low and the voice is forward, you will feel the tingling sensation on your lips.

You may be able to *feel* this hum when you say 'Many men make much money', 'homme, farmm, hamm', lingering on the 'hum' in these words. If you can do this, then the tone of voice is forward and more resonant.

2. Place fingertips on the larynx whilst you hum and feel the tingling on your lips, and count up to ten or say a simple phrase in your loudest voice and at the same time concentrate on the feeling on the finger tips.

3. The same procedure as Step 1 and Step 2 only using a quiet tone (but not whispering). Concentrate on the difference in feel on the fingertips.

The aim is to be aware of the contrast between a voice volume that is too loud in ordinary circumstances and the voice volume that is suitable for ordinary conversation but using *feeling* instead of (or as well as) hearing to monitor the loudness.

Repeated regular practice may be needed to establish this awareness. A friend can be invaluable in helping you to establish and recognize the loudness needed for ordinary conversation in quiet circumstances. A sound-level meter could be a substitute for the friend but is not so useful for stage 4.

At the end of the exercise have a short period of conversation while you concentrate on the fingertips on your larynx and on feeling the right degree of voice volume, your friend keeping check for you on the right amount of voice volume and indicating if it becomes too loud or too quiet.

Pronunciation

New words and phrases tumble into the language from all sorts of sources. (There is more about this fascinating subject in Chapter 9, 'Living Language'.) If you see new words written and are not sure of the pronunciation because you have not heard the word or phrase used, check the pronunciation with friends – they do not have to be experts at phonetics to tell you what the word rhymes with – then bring it into your own conversation with confidence.

There are some classic examples of words which are spelt very differently from the way they sound – everyday words like 'through' and 'threw'. Here are a few proper names where spelling can be misleading:

Cholmondley – pronounced *Chum*-lee
Colquhoun – pronounced Co-*hoon*.
Kirkcudbright – pronounced Kir-*coo*-brie.
Cirencester – sometimes called *Cis*sy-ter.

Different language may differ phonetically, for example the lovely sound like a soft gargle when a Scottish person says 'au*ch* the lo*ch*' is also used in Danish but is not used in England. The French do not go in for diphthongs but have at least one vowel sound that almost defeats the Anglo-Saxon.

Recently I met a speechreader who was struggling to understand a lady who spoke English with a French accent. Once they both switched to speaking in French, the problems were solved!

So far as I know, there is nothing anywhere which is like the sound

Welsh people make when they talk about *Lloyd* who lives at *Ll*andudno!

Once upon a time there was a film with a jolly popular song, sung as a duet. It enshrined a golden nugget of truth:

> You say potAYtoes
> and I say potAHtoes.
> You say tomAYtoes
> and I say tomAHtoes
> potAYtoes
> potAHtoes
> tomAYtoes
> tomAHtoes
> Let's call the whole thing off!

The message of this popular song is that sounds are used by different people in different ways. How they are used depends on accent, language, locality or simply the way people talk.

It is the SOUNDS you speechread. You learn by doing, because you have been talking for a long time. You already have the experience built in. Enjoy talking not only with people but even to yourself, your plants and your dog.

Many exercises on pages 190 to 193 are useful whether or not you have hearing loss.

8. Speechreading with High-Frequency Hearing Loss (HFHL)

Definition

This is loss of hearing mainly for the high-pitched sounds; sometimes the low-pitched sounds are little affected. Sounds such as traffic, footsteps and noise may be heard well, but sounds like the flute, telephone bell or kitten's mew may be missed altogether. A man's voice will be heard better than a woman's voice.

Human hearing has a tremendous range both in degree of loudness (what is just audible to what is painfully loud) and in frequency (the span between low-pitched sounds and the high-pitched sounds at the top of the scale). Some animals have an even greater range and can

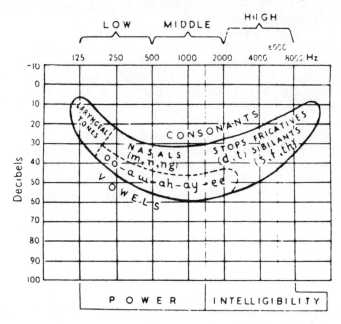

The frequency components of English speech sounds.[12]

hear sounds well above those heard by human beings.

The chart shows the frequency components of English speech. Reading from left to right, you will see that it is the lower register of speech which is concerned with power/volume and the high register with intelligibility.

Causes of high-frequency hearing loss (HFHL)

The ear consists of three parts: (1) the outer ear, which you can see, (2) the middle ear which acts as a conductor of sound to (3) the inner ear from which the message is conveyed to the brain. When the cause of deafness is not solely in the outer and/or middle ear, high frequencies are likely to be affected.

There are various causes of damage to the inner ear – for example, exposure to loud noise.

As age increases, the inner ear becomes less sensitive to high frequencies. This is normally a gradual process; few people notice that after the age of twenty-three they no longer hear the high-pitched squeak of a bat. Loss of high frequencies is usually unnoticed until sounds in the speech range are involved.

Different names are used to describe high-frequency hearing loss. Known as sensori neural deafness, it may have been called nerve deafness, perceptive deafness, inner ear deafness, presbyacusis – but by any name it is a frustrating type of hearing loss, at present not helped by surgery but undoubtedly helped by using sight together with listening tactics.

It is the consonant sounds which make speech intelligible; therefore it is not surprising that people who lose the high frequencies tend to hear the voice but not to be able to distinguish words. Increasing the loudness of voice will not necessarily give greater clarity. There comes a point where increased loudness results in reduced clarity.

When consonant clues are fewer, it takes longer to translate what is said into sense, but this does not mean that one's brain is slower! It means that it has fewer aural clues from which to decipher the sense.

Background noise may entirely obliterate the consonant sounds. Face-to-face conversation in quiet circumstances may be easy, but group chatter or background noise may make it impossible to understand the speaker. Much depends on acoustics. A reverberant place such as a church, empty hall or tiled kitchen is less easy than a room with some sound-absorbent furnishings, such as heavy curtains and thick carpet.

Exercises in HF sounds

To *see* what you cannot hear, particularly consonant sounds, improves speech reception wonderfully.

In your SAS practice you have already concentrated on consonants. Three in particular are easily missed or confused, even with slight HFHL, but are totally different when seen/felt. Say aloud at normal speed: 'Me*th*ylated *spirits* are not o*f*ten e*ff*erve*s*cent, are *th*ey?' Notice the sound/appearance/sensation. Compare the teeth-together hiss as you say 'The Mi*ss*i*ss*ippi flow*s* *s*wiftly to the *s*ea' to the lower-lip-to-top-teeth of 'The mu*ff*ins *f*ell onto the *f*loor' and to 'Judi*th*'s *th*ird bir*th*day is on *Th*ursday.'

In the sentences that follow, these sounds are used in pairs for comparison in your SAS practice (at normal speed, of course).

'Can you pay the *fees*?'
'Is he over*seas*?'

'Is that *fur* mink or rabbit?'
'Sorry *Sir*! It wasn't me, it was her.'

'Have a *sip* of brandy.'
'That's a *fib*, and you're a liar.'

This time compare the hiss in the first sentence with what you feel and see in the second.

'My heart *sank* when I saw the hill.'
'Please do *thank* Mary for the party.'

'He's miserable as *sin*.'
'She's looking very *thin*.'

'Hello! Here comes *Cecil*.'
'Ouch! I've trodden on a *thistle*.'

Compare sentences to which one more HF sound is added:

'A *posie* of wild flowers.'
'Please will you *throw* the ball.'
'They walked to and *fro* in the twilight.'
'Will you *sew* on my button?'

'She's a *pawn* in the game.'
'I've a *thorn* in my finger.'
'He's *sawn* up the logs.'

'A *fawn* is frollicking in the front garden.'

'The *paint* is wet. Don't touch.'
'Who is the patron *saint* of Wales?'
'She's going to *faint*. Get the smelling-salts.'
'Was the *Thane* of Wessex harassed by the Danes?'

The speaker

It is particularly true in HFHL that much depends on the speaker. In fact, people often articulate consonants better when they whisper!

Abnormal dislike of loud sounds is usual with this type of hearing loss. A sound which causes no discomfort to normal ears may seem unpleasant or painfully loud. Many hearing-aids have devices to restrict the loudness received by the aid user and also to provide tone selection, but there are still aid users who find that sound volume must be reduced in noisy circumstances. Binaural listening – with an aid in each ear – may increase tolerance of noise and provide better intelligibility of speech. In extreme cases a hearing-aid may be useless.

It is helpful if the speaker has good articulation (crisp consonants) and is able to phrase sentences so that the key word or subject does not depend on a high frequency – for example, instead of saying 'Do you know Sussex?' (key word Sussex), they could say 'Have you been in this part of the world before?'

The very elderly

Senior citizens frequently experience high-frequency hearing loss. If speechreading is being considered for someone who is very elderly, it should be recognized that it is only one of many factors.

Elderly people may become socially isolated because of the lessening of family ties, bereavement, physical infirmity, restricted mobility and ever-increasing difficulties of transport. Communication skills not used deteriorate. Opportunities for communication may have been reduced; the concentration needed to listen attentively may be for shorter periods; the whole process of comprehension and response may have slowed down. There may be physical and other handicaps such as impaired sight or poor memory.[13]

The speaker may need to be physically closer, to use the reassuring sense of touch, to remember that the whole face and expression help to convey meaning, to express one thought at a time unhurriedly, at the pace suitable to the old person. Social isolation may be reduced when a small group of people share a common interest or activity which stimulates conversation.

Elderly citizens have a fund of experience and knowledge. In this age when many people are adrift and searching for their roots, the elderly can provide stability, experience and wisdom. If we can take positive action to improve communication, then the whole community will benefit.

9. Living Language

How people express themselves in words

Spoken language is what you speechread. It is not only how a person speaks that matters to the speechreader; it is also the language he uses.

You have already noticed that some people speak more clearly than others, but this chapter is not about good articulation. It is about something even more important: the way in which people express their thoughts.

Spoken language is living, flexible and rich in its variation. It reflects the society and the times we live in as well as having roots which go deep down into history. It not only reveals much about the speaker: it also influences him. It is never dull or static. People do not talk in written English but in living, colloquial, personal language. It is people *talking* that you are going to see.

You will see people not only stating facts, asking questions and giving information but airing opinions, expressing their feelings, sharing their experiences, thinking aloud. People talk for all sorts of reasons – to express emotions, to 'let off steam', to impress other people, to be the life and soul of the party to instruct and inform. Some use words as a smoke-screen to hide their meaning or their feelings. Some chat for hours to their dog; some talk to plants, and of course some people talk for fun, because they like doing it.

What people say is not necessarily concise, direct, factual or precise, but a message gets through. If what is said is contradicted by what is seen – that is when the words do not 'match' the facial expression – then, to the astute observer, it is the words which will be disregarded, and what is seen will be believed.

Repetition

Repetition in everyday conversation can be a mixed blessing if one is trying to grasp meaning – if only people would come to the point!

Some people use one overworked phrase frequently. Interviews with 'the man in the street' may sound something like this: 'Well, I mean to say – I mean, I really don't think … it doesn't make sense, I mean. Well, does it, I mean. I mean you really wouldn't yourself, not you yourself, I mean, if it was you, I mean …' See what I mean?

If people express their thoughts intermingled with plentiful 'ums' and 'ers', you have probably grasped their meaning anyway before they complete the sentence.

A foreigner once said to me, 'In order to speak English you must learn one word thoroughly.' Can you spot the word in this conversation? See if you can imagine the sort of person who said it: 'My dear, how nice to see you. Have you had a nice holiday? How nice! Did you meet the Joneses? Such nice people. I'm glad the weather was nice, makes all the difference, nice weather. Must go now, darling. I'm taking Fido for a nice walkie because it's such a nice day. Diddems have nice walkie walkie den? He knows every word I say! He's wagging his tail! Nice boy den. Bye now – have a nice day.'

The same thought is expressed differently in different circumstances.

Mr Smith is a politician. At a public meeting he might say something like this:

> … and in the short space of time allocated to me I would like you to know that this is an occasion at which I am indeed proud – extremely proud – to be present. [Applause] I can only say, and say again, that as you move forward, we are right behind you.
>
> I am here to underline [pause], to confirm [pause], to tell you with the utmost conviction [longish pause] that because we are behind you, the basic situation is that we move forward [slight pause] together. [Loud applause.]

At a previous consultation committee, Mr Smith probably said something like: 'In support of the proposal, there is no doubt that the policy of co-operation is essential, but I would like to sound a note of caution to ensure certain inbuilt safeguards of reasonable limitation of commitment.' (All you really need is 'co-operation with safeguards'.)

Later on, in a pub, Mr Smith chats to a friend: 'Of course we've got to get stuck in, at least to some extent, because the alternatives make the mind boggle.'

Now let's eavesdrop on old Bill.

'I say Charlie, a little bird told me that Joe there's been a bit crafty. Remember that garden fork he borrowed? He's been and gone and sold it! Honest he has! Of all the blooming cheek! Sold it! He just about takes the biscuit. It's about time Joe pulled himself together. He talks a lot of tommy rot about not making ends meet, but what I say is you've got to cut your coat according to your cloth. That's what I say.'

Conversational speech

Think of the very different way in which people express themselves in a bedtime story, a lecture, in giving directions, making announcements, making an after-dinner speech. These activities are not the same as speech used for conversation.

In conversational speech the two-way element is crucial. The conversation grows through mutual contributions. Each person can direct and manipulate the conversation to some extent. If the 'feedback' process shows that the subject is not acceptable to the other person, it may be dropped or modified or changed.

The kind of vocabulary depends on the person speaking. It may be influenced by his upbringing, age, social environment, family background, intelligence, education, interests and of course his job and where he lives.

Jargon

Different kinds of jargon are used by people in different jobs or professions, and are associated with different hobbies and groups of people. The expressions used by the budgie-fancier are different from those of the judo enthusiast. The lawyer, the space-game expert, the physicist and the young man on his motor-bike may be almost unintelligible to each other when using the 'in' words and expressions of their particular group, unless the 'lingo' is already known.

What sports, hobbies or groups are you in touch with? Make a list of the special words and phrases which are used, put them into sentences and weave them thoroughly into the do-it-yourself SAS mirror-practice with which you are still persevering faithfully and regularly every day. (If you are not, then please stop reading this book and begin at once.)

Observe the speaker

Do not be limited by seeing only what is said. Notice who is saying it. Suppose Mrs Bloggs is ill-treated by Mr Bloggs but decides to put up with this situation because of the children. The neighbour might say: 'He goes for her something shocking, but she sticks him because of the kids.' A social worker could sum it up as: 'Mr Bloggs is immature, overcompensating by asserting his status in the family. Emotionally unstable, his aggressive attitude frequently culminates in violence. Mrs Bloggs plays a passive role, adjusting to the situation. She has become somewhat withdrawn. Supportive help is needed to sustain the personality of the children.' One of the children might say, 'Coo, innit good. Good ole mum – innit good.' 'Innit' is not in the dictionary, but it is said and understood.

Can you put the following condensed words into sentences? Strew snot snit water sad snow yup mup.

Answers:
Strew, every word of it.
Snot possible! I just don't believe it.
Snit nice today? Snit bad luck! Snit a shame!
Water pity!
Sad its day. We'll have to throw it away.
Snow use. It's too late to alter it now.
No. 7 is what mother calls upstairs every morning at 7 a.m.
No. 8 is what her daughter shouts downstairs in reply.
'Sow e sesit' is what you see.
'Sow lie fizz, snit?' (Say this aloud and the meaning is clear through SAS.)

Spoken language grows and changes

New words appear, old ones may change their meaning. New sayings are on everyone's lips for a few years and then for no reason they disappear, becoming as dead and as dated as the dodo.

P.G. Wodehouse captured some of the 'in' words of the early twenties, the 'golly! topping, ripping, whackho! Toodleoo, toodlepip, rightho!' reflecting the age of the 'flapper' – and how dated these expressions sound today! The Second World War introduced many new sayings: 'wizard prang' which became 'wizard', 'do a pancake' and 'put me in the picture'. 'Oh boy, am I with it.' 'Come up and see me sometime.'

More recently came teddy-boys, mods and rockers, with words like 'terrific', 'smashing', 'fantastic', 'bang-on' and 'I'm alright, Jack'. Skinheads and Punks appeared, using their own jargon – there were Hells Angels and four-letter words (incidentally, I'm still wondering what these words are!). Things were 'fabulous'. As I write, one of the overworked words is 'basically', and that tedious word 'problem' is still as rampant as ever. Out of curiosity I counted the times that 'problem' cropped up in a town plan document. It went into double figures on the first page. Even the local shoe-shop has a notice outside saying, 'We deal with shoe-repair problems.'

'Radio' and 'stereo' are 'in' – 'wireless' is out. Ladies no longer wear 'coats and skirts', instead they go for 'suits', 'separates' or 'mix and match'. 'Frocks' have largely been replaced by 'dresses'. Until recent times 'gay' meant happy – now it has different usage. How misleading such changes can be unless one keeps up to date! Years ago there was a drawing-room, dining-room, sitting-room and study, a kitchen and scullery; now there is a living-room, lounge, breakfast area or open-plan and patio. Hard wear or soft wear referred to tweed, not to electronics. There were no yuppies or floppy discs.

Some words become shortened: (tele)phone, (re)frig(erator), (in)flu(enza) and (omni)bus, to name but a few. Others become lengthened – words like 'transport' changed to 'transportation'.

Pronunciation changes too

The word 'garage', for instance, used to sound more like 'g'rahge', almost said as one syllable. The accent then moved itself onto the first syllable ('*gar*rage'), and now the pronunciation is sometimes changed to '*gar*ridge'.

These changes are absorbed almost without noticing. They are usually overheard and slip into our own use without any effort or thought. When hearing loss is severe, this is not so easy, for changes may not be automatically absorbed.

Keep your memory-bank up to date

This can be done in many ways. It helps to be aware of the living nature of language and to be interested in the subject.

If you come across an unfamiliar word or phrase, find its source. Perhaps it is too new to appear in reference books. Do you meet it in the newspaper? Do your friends use it? Can they tell you, when they use it, what it expresses for them? Will you include it in future when you are talking? Do you need to check pronunciation?

Why not make a list of words and expressions which are recent. It is hard to imagine that not so very long ago there were no words for sellotape, instant-mix, deep-freeze, TV, drip-dry, silicon chip or jet-lag.

Colloquial expressions

Colloquial speech comes into conversation – another reason why one should grasp the meaning of whole sentences and not try to take words literally.

Many expressions are stored in your memory-bank already. Say the following sentences up to time and you may have little difficulty in including the missing words shown by the dots.

1. ... like a trooper	12. Pig and ...
2. ... like a stone	13. Dustpan and ...
3. ... like a fish	14. ... and polish
4. As ... as ditchwater	15. ... and early
5. As ... as a picture	16. Here today and ...
6. As ... as a mouse	17. Faith, hope and ...
7. As hungry as a ...	18. Red white and ...
8. As quick as ...	19. Snow White and ...
9. As snug as ...	20. Laugh ... laughs with ... Weep ... alone.
10. As miserable as ...	21. Red sky in the morning ...
11. Cup and ...	

Answers: 1. swear 2. sink 3. drink 4. dull 5. pretty 6. quiet 7. hunter 8. a flash (or lightning) 9. a bug in a rug 10. sin 11. saucer 12. whistle 13. brush 14. spit 15. bright 16. gone tomorrow 17. charity 18. blue 19. the seven dwarfs 20. and the world ... you ... and you weep ... 21. ... shepherd's warning.

In your do-it-yourself practice, put one or two well-known phrases or sentences together as SAS exercises (at normal-pace speech of course). For example: 'I'd better get up bright and early today. There's a lot to do.' 'Touch my toes a few times first. Better keep fit as a fiddle and ready for anything.' 'I hope there's a fat cheque in the post, otherwise I shall be as poor as a church mouse. That'll be a fine kettle of fish and no mistake.'

Sources

It is important to remember the metaphorical and symbolic richness of the English language; and therefore to guard against taking language too literally. Many sources of the living languages are ancient. Some currently used are from the Bible and Prayer Book – phrases like: 'I have played the fool', 'The apple of my eye', 'Eat, drink and be merry, for tomorrow we die.'

In the past, human beings lived closer to, and were much more in touch with, nature. This is reflected in some of the expressions which include animals. Someone may be referred to as mulish, a vixen, a shrew, dogged, cowed. They may fight like a lion or go at something like a bull at a gate. They may be eagle-eyed or watch like a lynx. They may be wise as an owl, slippery as an eel or even a snake in the grass. You will notice phrases like crocodile tears, the elephant never forgets, and the ostrich burying its head in the sand.

What other expressions can you think of which include the name of an animal? You will enjoy beavering away to find out.

Ways of conveying meaning

Meaning can be conveyed in subtle ways: through tone of voice, pauses, stress given to different words or syllables, and even by what is left unsaid, by what is inferred or implied. Being aware of this, you will be alert and attentive to meaning. You will use your powers of anticipation and imagination to read between the lines, to understand message and meaning.

We have all met the person who expresses himself or herself indirectly – 'Well, of course I would, but it's George – you know how it is ... It's not that I don't want to ... I do hope you'll find someone else ... such a shame ... you know old George! Need I say more!' Someone in the kitchen may not say, 'Put this bowl inside the bigger bowl which you will find on the top shelf of the green cupboard.' She may say, 'Put that in the other one in there.'

Tone of voice cannot be seen. The eyes may reveal much. Here is a simple sentence: 'Will you come with me?' Think of it being said by a policeman who adds, 'We think you may be able to help us in our enquiries.' The same words will be said very differently by Romeo when discussing the future schedule with Juliet. Tone of voice and stressed words can change the sentence to a command, a request, a question, an invitation.

Here is a simple statement: 'Mary comes to Eastbourne by train.' If the stress is on 'Mary', this may imply that Elizabeth doesn't. With stress on 'comes', could it be that she gets a lift back? With the stress on 'Eastbourne', the speaker may go on to say that she travels to Bexhill by bus.

Another simple sentence: 'Will you have another helping of trifle?' Which words might be stressed to indicate, 'Or would you prefer jelly?', 'Isn't that a bit greedy?', 'I'm not asking Mary'.

Meaning wrapped up in waffle

Meaning may be wrapped in so many layers of words or unnecessary phrases that it almost disappears. Expressions like, 'at this moment in time', 'in this day and age', 'part and parcel' may be practised so that they are recognized and ignored.

How much easier to speechread. 'Nothing is happening at present' than to interpret into sense 'Basically the situation is static, not advancing or regressing but stagnant.' When pointing out that someone keeps quiet because he wants to make a good impression, why not say so? It is really more to the point than 'maintaining a low profile when projecting his image'.

When the controller of a space rocket said recently that the team were going to decide what to do next, he expressed the thought as, 'We will evaluate the situation in order to make a determination.' The financial wizard talks about 'margins being squeezed on a contracting market; controlled inputs stabilizing capital have reached the ceiling', and he assures us that, 'The Treasury mandarins would put Britain into a straitjacket, paying the price for decades before the recession bottoms out.' I wonder what he means? I don't know – does *he*? Obscure forms of expression prevent speechreading unless they are already familiar. Understanding is not conveyed solely through clear diction but has a lot to do with the language used.

The tabloid English of newspapers is a good example of how different the written word can be from the spoken. Who would ever say: 'Boy suspended by Head, Top Prof. slams system', when what they mean is that a pupil has been sent home by his headmaster and some well-known professor doesn't think that is a good idea?

Some words are onomatopoeic. That is, they convey by sound what they describe – words such as scrunch, squelch, murmur, ting-a-ling, squidgy, howl, crunchy, yuk and footsteps that go pitter-patter or just clump, clump, clump. Can you think of others?

Clichés can misdirect the speechreader's train of thought. A speechreader was chatting about roses to a keen gardener. Suddenly he said 'If that manure doesn't do the trick for my yellow mermaids, I'm a Dutchman.' My friend had 'got the message' – realized his roses were called yellow mermaids but was puzzled by the end of the sentence. 'I'm a Dutchman,' he repeated. 'A what?' 'A Dutchman,' he shouted. Oh dear!

Now you put your shoulder to the wheel, your nose to the grindstone, your best foot forward and your back to the wall to see how many clichés you know and how they are to be interpreted or ignored.

Accents and dialect

The way people pronounce words presents little difficulty; it is the *sounds* which you see. You 'hear' the sounds in your mind's ear, developed through all that SAS practice.

'Hello,' said Linda. 'Where do you come from?' 'I live here,' said Jason, 'but you come from Scotland, don't you?' They both relied solely on speechreading; it was their first meeting.

'Have some more tea,' said a stranger. 'Thanks,' John replied. 'You're a Londoner, aren't you?' John had spotted the Cockney pronunciation of the word 'tea', though he relied solely on speechreading. Would people with sharp ears have been so perceptive?

When dialect is a matter of different words being used, naturally it will be understood only if it is known previously.

If a Scot says: 'It's a couthy wee but 'n ben. The lum reeks brawly' – the sentence can be heard/seen/felt but will not click into sense unless the language is familiar. The same applies if an Australian says: 'Don't come the raw prawns on me. Rattle your dags. I'm after big bikkies.' Some Australian idiom reflects the Cockney rhyming slang: 'Noah's ark' for shark, or 'Have a Captain Cook' for look.

Cockneys are well known for rhyming slang. 'That's a smart pair of daisies' (daisy root = boots); 'She's me old Dutch' (Duchess of Fife = wife); 'Use your crust' (crust of bread = head) – more widespread now as 'Use your loaf.'

American English may use the same words as 'English' English, but with a different meaning. An 'undershirt' means a vest, and a 'vest' means a waistcoat. Better study this further before meeting those American cousins with cookies and candy.

Enough of this blether! But enough, I hope, to start you searching for more.

Many ways of expressing the same thought

Imagine who would use the particular form below. Imagine the question to which they are replying. Then add to the list.

Ways of saying Yes
 Absolutely
 Without a shadow of doubt
 Agreed
 Of course
 I will
 That's right
 Why not!
 Definitely
 If you like
 Not half
 Every time
 You try and stop me
 Love to
 Sure
 Right you are
 That would be lovely

Ways of saying No
 Nope
 Not today, thank you
 Thank you, no
 Drop dead
 Not me
 Get lost
 Rather not, thanks
 Not a hope
 Never in a month of Sundays
 No way
 Over my dead body

Not on your life
I don't approve
You must be joking!
My wife won't let me
My husband would never allow it

Ways of saying Perhaps:
 Everything is in the balance at present.
 Not possible to give a decision at this
  moment in time.
 All very uncertain at this juncture.
 Wait and see.
 Let you know in due course.
 Neither here nor there.
 Well, that all depends ...
 Time will tell.
 I shall have to ask my mother first.
 Well, we don't have to decide now,
  do we?

Ways of saying 'Don't know':
 Search me!
 Ask me another!
 Neither here nor there.
 Six-of-one and half-a-dozen of the other.
 Haven't a clue! Haven't the foggiest!
 Regrettably I am unable to give a
  decisive opinion.
 It's problematical.
 Sorry, I'm a stranger here.

Material for DIY practice

The people you meet every day talk in ordinary everyday language: you grasp the message and meaning. Great literature and oratory can be useful in another way, affording the material for do-it-yourself practice. The emphasis, rhythm, inflection, tone of voice and above all the natural pauses convey more than their factual meaning. By memorizing short passages and by relishing them and using them frequently in your do-it-yourself SAS training, your speech reading will improve and your aural memory-bank will be enriched.

Experiment by comparing the following two different statements about the same facts.

In 1940 the United Kingdom, with no defences, faced what seemed to be certain invasion by hostile armed forces. An official announcement could have been made as follows: 'Imminent invasion by superior forces is expected in the near future. In spite of regrettable, but unavoidable, lack of defences, it is recommended that vigorous resistance is displayed on all occasions rather than capitulation.' In the event the message was delivered rather differently as follows: '... We shall defend our island, whatever the cost may be. We shall fight on the beaches. We shall fight on the landing grounds. We shall fight in the fields and in the streets. We shall fight in the hills. We shall never surrender.'

Compare these two statements in your do-it-yourself mirror practice. Memorize and then say them in the way that moves you emotionally, noticing the sound (or memory of sound), the appearance and the sensation as you say them aloud.

The first statement is a somewhat flat flow of words with only one pause. In the second statement every short group of simple words creates a picture, has its own emphasis and rhythm. Say the whole piece with unhurried determination. It is not difficult to understand why this short statement by Winston Churchill changed history. Find similar short pieces, enjoy them, memorize them, say them often in your SAS practice, say them often to yourself. Relish them.

Finally, there are various reference books you may wish to keep handy and dip into: Roget's *Thesaurus*, Brewer's *Dictionary of Phrase and Fable*, *The Oxford Book of English Usage*, *A Dictionary of Clichés*, *The Penguin Dictionary of Quotations*, *The Penguin Dictionary of Historical Slang* and of course a good dictionary which includes derivations and pronunciation of words.

There are some books which are written in spoken language, books like *Tom Forrest's Country Calendar* – a chat or paper by a countryman in his own words. *Let stalk strine* is full of people who talk in Australian English. Another little book, *Krek Waiter's speak Bristle*, is written in sounds as they are heard – not as they are spelt (easily understood when said aloud using your aural memory combined with the sensation and the appearance of speech). Your friendly library will recommend other books, I feel sure.

Crosswords and games such as Lexicon or Scrabble may all increase your word power. In conclusion, try this puzzle in which everyday expressions are illustrated. Everyday language, yes, but the words should not be taken literally.

Can you identify the article, condition or saying in each box?

Afterwards check your answers with those overpage

1	2	3
JACK	MAN —— BOARD	STAND I

4	5	6
T O W N	R O ROADS D S	WEAR —— LONG

7	8	9
CYCLE CYCLE CYCLE	 iiii	THE HOTOADLE

10	11	12
MIND —— MATTER	HE'S HIM SELF	DEATH LIFE

13	14	15
c.u.	IQ	PRESCRIPTION "

16	17	18
VISION VISION	⬜ (circle)	GROUND FEET FEET FEET FEET FEET FEET

19	20	21
$\frac{1}{8}$	C O S S T	KNEE LIGHTS

Answers

1. Jack-in-a-box
2. Man overboard
3. I understand
4. Downtown
5. Crossroads
6. Long underwear
7. Tricycle
8. Spots before the eyes
9. Toad-in-the-hole
10. Mind over matter
11. He's beside himself
12. Life after death
13. See you!
14. Low IQ
15. Repeat prescription
16. Double vision
17. Square peg in a round hole
18. Six feet underground
19. One over the eight
20. Rising costs
21. Neon lights

10.　Further Practice Suggestions

What I hear, I forget.

What I see, I remember.

What I experience I understand.

Knowing the subject talked about, knowing the context, using language sense, anticipation and aural memory are strong foundations for speechreading skills. In past chapters exercises have been suggested to encourage speed of response when the subject and situation are known. It is vital that you continue your 'learn by doing' work. This chapter may be useful back-up material but ONLY if used with the up-to-time normal speech. In the following exercises the situation is known, but there is a very wide choice of subject. Practise only for short periods, never when you are tired.

No. 1

The *unchanging* first part of the sentence (spoken *normally*) is always: 'I went into the garden and I found ...' There are many different ways of completing the sentence. Your practice partner has prepared some of them like this:

I went into the garden and I found it was pouring with rain.

I went into the garden and I found the cat up a tree.

I went into the garden and I found the baby was asleep in the pram.

I went into the garden and I found the washing had blown away.

I went into the garden and I found the wheelbarrow was full of rubbish.

You reply at once if you get the meaning the first time ('Did you get wet? Did you call the fire brigade?' and so on). If you do not reply, the PP *does not repeat* but goes on to the next question. After five questions you are handed the list to read before they are repeated by PP, and you reply to (but never repeat) what has been said.

Pause before following with another five sentences.

This particular exercise can be done in many ways, always up to time, *always* with the first part of the sentence unchanged, although the second part is different:

I came into the room and it was full of smoke ... and I fell over the mat ... and no one noticed ... and switched on the light ... and the party was in full swing.

or again:

I looked out of the window and I saw the postman delivering letters.

I looked out of the window and I saw a queue of people waiting for the bus ... and so on.

or again:

There's someone at the door – see who it is.

There's someone at the door – if it's Mrs Brown, say I'm out.

There's someone at the door – it's probably the gas man.

The set part of the sentence should be about the same length as the variable part which is used to finish it. Never use only one word; always use the complete sentence; always talk at normal pace, without exaggeration, PP always use your voice – but speak quietly.

No. 2

The subject and situation are unknown, but this time the set sentence is followed by a shorter, unknown portion in which there are two clues. If you get one of them, your may anticipate the other.

When the sentence is said by PP (*said*, never read), you immediately respond. Whether or not you have understood (say 'Pass', if not), the next question is asked. At the end of five sentences you look at the list.

Say the sentences yourself (sound/appearance/sensation).

PP says the sentences again but in the same order (and you respond to each), then the same ten sentences in random order.

Here are ten sentences:

1. Where would I find a loaf of bread?
2. Where would I find a load of rubbish?
3. Where would I find a bunch of grapes?
4. Where would I find a box of matches?
5. Where would I find a ball of string?
6. Where would I find a bottle of wine?
7. Where would I find a sack of potatoes?
8. Where would I find a crowd of people?
9. Where would I find a cluster of stars?
10. Where would I find a flock of sheep?

Having grasped the principle of these exercises, you will want to make your own lists, but it is vitally important to follow the form suggested and that normal speech is used.

No. 3

In this exercise, in addition to grasping the whole sentence, you have to think quickly before replying.

Please can you tell me what has a lip but no mouth?

Please can you tell me what has a mouth but no lip?

Continue to repeat the unchanging part of the sentence, but the different endings could be: teeth but no mouth? ... an eye but no sight? ... hands but no arms? ... legs but no feet? ... a neck but no head? ... skin but no bones? ... a core but no heart? ... arms but no hands?

1. Jug. 2. River. 3. Comb. 4. Potato. Needle. Storm. 5. Clock. 6. Chair. 7. Bottle. 8. Orange. Banana, etc. 9. Apple. 10. Chair.

Answers

No. 4

An advanced one this! There is no context to help you.

The unchanging first part of the sentence is always: What country or people do you think of when the conversation is about ...? What country or people do you think of when the conversation is about boomerangs?

Continuing to use the unchanging first part of the sentence, the different endings could be: lotus flowers? ... pyramids? ... whisky? ... tulips? ... shamrock? ... chopsticks? ... tomahawks? ... clogs? ... coffee? You respond: Australia, India, Egypt (and so on).

No. 5

Is similar but this time the unchanging part of the sentence is: What nationality do you think of when I say ...?

The changed part of the sentence at the end could be: ... when I say ice cream? ... when I say oranges? ... when I say vodka? ... when I say thistles? ... when I say macaroni? ... when I say opium? ... when

I say sombrero? ... when I say rickshaw? ... when I say watches? ... when I say beret?

On no account feel despondent if you find these exercises difficult – they are! But using them in exactly the way suggested will increase your skills. Be sure the *whole* sentence, up-to-time, is used. Have a look at the list before the sentences are repeated again, first in the same order and then in random order. Always take a pause after five sentences.

No. 6

This follows the same original principle. Set beginning of sentence: What would you find in a ...? – a garden shed? ... a shopping-basket? ... a washing-machine? ... a thermos flask? ... a wine bottle? ... and so on.

You will notice that some questions were somewhat easier because there were longer words involved. Longer words are easier to see than short ones. 'Pomposity' is easier than 'kit-kat' or 'ice-cream'. The rhythm of the whole sentence carries the meaning forward.

No. 7

This follows the same principle and method of application. The first unchanging part of the sentence is always: Please can you tell me where to buy ...? The sentence finishes with: a newspaper? ... an overcoat? ... a goldfish? ... writing paper? ... a television set? ... an alarm clock? ... an engagement ring?

The possibilities of this type of exercise are endless, but it must always be used *in the right way* in order to help you press forward into even more effective speechreading.

No. 8

Now we are changing the form of exercise but with the same principle of grasping the situation and the message from a few clues.

This time your PP says: I went shopping and bought a toothbrush. I went shopping and bought a toothbrush and a bar of soap. I went shopping and bought a toothbrush and a bar of soap and a face flannel.

When (and only when) five items have accumulated by being added at the end of the previous complete sentence, you reply with the type of shop – in this case obviously a chemist's shop.

Do not reply until all five items have been listed in the way suggested above.

Continue this exercise with items in a stationer's, bakery, ironmonger's, fish shop and so on.

No. 9

Your PP makes statements about his surroundings, then you find out where he is. Always the three statements are in the same order with the identical first part of the sentence. For example: Where am I?

I can see water all around me.
I can smell the ozone.
I can feel sea breezes.

The answer might be on the pier or in a boat.

I can see the mixing-bowl and wooden spoon.
I can smell the cake in the oven.
I can feel the warmth from the oven.

The answer is likely to be in the kitchen.

Do not reply until the end of the third sentence. If you find you are not 'in the right place', then look at the written statements and ask PP to say them again now that you know what to expect. (PP must always speak naturally and up to time, otherwise these exercises are useless.)

No. 10

The speed speechreader using the natural method aims to grasp whole sentences, the 'synthetic' approach. What if the subject is unknown?

Part A of Exercise 10 is to help you to discover the subject from the recognition of possible clues. This exercise should *not be attempted* until you have first acquired the firm foundations outlined earlier, and it is essential to use the material in the exact way suggested.

Part A. PP says ten single words from a prepared list with a pause between each. Possibly by the time PP has completed the list you will have grasped the subject; you may even get it before word ten.

Always you see the written list after the tenth word and then go through the list again with your PP (never repeating the individual word of course, but knowing the subject you will now find the words easier to recognize).

Part B. Use the same lists of words. Put each in turn into a well-known saying or into a sentence – you and your PP can take it in turns as you go down the list saying the set word followed by a sentence which the word stimulates you to think about.

If you read the list first, you will destroy the usefulness of the exercise. This is why groups of ten words are listed on page 114. One group is shown below so that you can see how the exercise works.

First part (A)	*Second part (B)*
Cat	The cat and the fiddle
Dog	Every dog has its day
Lion	Daniel in the lion's den
Horse	That's a horse of another colour
Donkey	Have you been to a donkey derby?
Rabbit	He will rabbit on instead of shutting up
Wolf	Keep the wolf from the door
Monkey	That child's a little monkey
Elephant	The elephant never forgets
Mouse	Poor as a church mouse

The following exercises start with a known word and explore where it may lead.

No. 11

1. Choose a much-used word. This is the key word of the exercise.
2. Think of ways in which it is used, in conjunction with another word or words. List them.
3. Describe in a short sentence what is meant by each word on your list, but *do not use* the key word in the description. Example: Let us suppose you decide upon the word 'out' (Step 1). You make your list of, say, ten or eleven examples (Step 2):

outlaw
outside
out-of-date
outline
look out
outgrow
outfitter
output
outstanding
phaseout
cutout
outhouse
outdoors

Describe what is meant in a short sentence (Step 3).

For example 'Something that has become old-fashioned'. (Yes – you will think and then reply, 'out-of-date' or 'outmoded'.)

The examples you have found should be used in your SAS practice.

The following suggestions are to start you off.

UP
uptight
wake-up
put-you-up
pin-up
up the pole
fed-up
shut up
hold up
mix up
make up
look up
ring up
turn up
upstart
worked up
give up
on the up and up
a put-up job etc

HAND
sleight of hand
in hand
handout
underhand
first hand
hand-in-glove
on the other hand etc

DOWN
down town
down under
down-trodden
upside down
down the hatch
down and out etc

OFF
off-beat
off-shore
write-off
carry-off
sign-off
spin-off
pay-off etc

HEAD
headland
headstrong
headlines
headband
headrest
hard-headed
head like a sieve
blockhead
headache
keeping your head above water etc

With a practice partner all you need to know is the key word chosen.

Your practice partner makes the list (which you do not see in advance) and then gives the short descriptive sentence which provides a clue to the way in which the key word has been used. A few descriptive sentences may be needed, but don't make it tedious by slowing things down. Better to look at the written key word, get your practice partner to repeat the descriptive sentences (which will then be easy) and go on to the next on the list. As usual do not repeat but always reply as quickly as possible.

No. 10 contd

List 1	*List 2*	*List 3*
1. Pears	Elm	Smarties
2. Figs	Holly	Toffee
3. Apples	Lilac	Chocolate
4. Grapes	Lime	Fruit drops
5. Gooseberries	Oak	Liquorice allsorts
6. Oranges	Laburnum	Toffee apple
7. Pineapple	Beech	Bullseyes
8. Banana	Silver Birch	Fudge
9. Melon	Mountain Ash	Lollipop
10. Peach	Cedar	Jelly baby

List 4	*List 5*	*List 6*
1. Hockey	Onions	Crow
2. Cricket	Carrots	Seagull (or Eagle)
3. Golf	Swedes	Robin
4. Tennis	Cabbage	Swan
5. Squash	Parsnips	Owl
6. Rugger	Brocolli	Albatross
7. Bowls	Brussels sprouts	Budgerigar
8. Badminton	Potato	Sparrow
9. Water Polo	Cucumber	Thrush
10. Baseball	Marrow	Blackbird

Even without a practice partner, you will enjoy this simple exercise, and you may be surprised how widely one little word is used in our language. This should be extended to include short colloquial phrases.

No. 12

Choose a particular key word. Practice partner uses set sentence (at normal speed of course): 'What do people mean when they say ...?' and finishes the sentence by including the key word.

Example: Key word: 'Fire'
What do people mean when they say, 'No smoke without fire'?
What do people mean when they say, 'He won't set the Thames on fire'?
What do people mean when they say, 'Spreads like wildfire'?

What do people mean when they say, 'Fiery personality'?

What do people mean when they say, 'Put your hand in the fire'?

What do people mean when they say, 'Out of the frying-pan, into the fire'?

What do people mean when they say, 'Fire away'?

What do people mean when they say, 'Misfire'?

Suppose the key word is 'Water':

What do people mean when they say, 'As weak as water'?

What do people mean when they say, 'A lot of water has gone under the bridge'?

What do people mean when they say, 'The excuse doesn't hold water'?

What do people mean when they say, 'Water it down a bit'?

What do people mean when they say, 'A watering place'?

Your response is to think quickly and reply. This is quite extraordinarily hard work. You may decide to see the entire list written down first and then to have the questions asked at random.

You can continue to pursue the key words in different directions, thinking of the various ways they can be used.

water vole
water rat
water weed
water beetle
water buttercup
water meadow

firefly
fire-engine
firework
firebrand
misfire
bush fire

Always speechread entire sentences, either from your practice partner or in your own learn-by-doing practice.

Now let us pause for a moment to think about two landmarks in Mrs O's progress.

A stranger had been chatting with Mrs O for some time. When she asked her opinion of a radio programme, Mrs O replied that, as she had total hearing loss, she didn't hear the programme. The stranger was flabbergasted. 'You can't possibly be deaf!' she said. 'You hear me perfectly.'

A few weeks later there was an even better moment. Mrs O had been chatting to a close friend for over an hour. Suddenly she realized that she had forgotten she was relying totally on speed speechreading.

No. 13

Make a list of objects to be found in one room; for example, 'Objects in the kitchen':

> butter dish
> breadboard
> jam spoon
> carving knife
> cake tin
> tea caddy
> milk jug
> cup and saucer
> sugar bowl
> coffee pot

Use this in two ways.

A. Where are they? Your PP tells you where the first five are, always starting with the object. This might be as follows:

> The butter dish is in the fridge.
> The breadboard is on the larder shelf.
> The jam spoon is in the jam pot.
> The carving knife is in the sideboard drawer.
> The tea caddy is on the kitchen table.

Then stop. PP asks questions, always including the key word: 'Where shall I find the jam spoon?' 'Where do you keep the carving knife?' and so on.

The next stage is to ask questions which do not include the key word.

'What is on the kitchen table?' or 'What is on the larder shelf?' etc. Continue with your next five sentences.

B. Think of a saying which includes the key word, or part of it. For example:

> Fine words butter no parsnips.
> Bread is the staff of life.
> Jam yesterday, jam tomorrow but never jam today.

It's balanced on a knife edge.

You can't have your cake and eat it.

Everything stops for tea.

The milk of human kindness.

We'll take a cup of kindness yet.

Have you a sugar daddy? (or of course it might be more appropriate to say, Are you a sugar daddy?)

Everything's gone to pot.

No. 14. Association of ideas

One word may lead to another, just as one topic of conversation may lead to another.

Suppose we choose the word 'light'. It may immediately make you think of 'candle' – 'power-cut' – 'strike' – 'inflation' – 'rising costs' – 'bank balance', or 'light' makes you think of 'long light evenings' – 'summertime' – 'gardening' – 'lumbago' – and so on.

PP asks: What saying is suggested when a person does not fuss about something? Yes, they 'make light of it'.

What saying is suggested when 'clothing is not heavy'? Yes – it's lightweight.

What is surrounded by water and gives warning to sailors of dangerous rocks? Yes, lighthouse, lightship.

No. 15

Descriptions of simple activities open a whole field for practice materials.

An activity is decided upon by your PP, but you do not know what it is. Your PP describes what happens in factual, direct sentences. After four or five different activities have been described, you read the list of activities. One of the activities (you don't know which) is then described again, not necessarily in the same words. Try to spot which of the four or five known activities it is.

Here are one or two activities as starting suggestions (you will think of many more): making bread – painting the ceiling – bathing the dog – writing a letter – mending a fuse – changing a lightbulb.

Discussions between two people provide good materials, but will be useless if words are mouthed, since, as ever, you need whole sentences at normal speed with normal rhythm. It is useful to sit at the corner of a small table (a card table is excellent) whilst your discussion partner sits at the opposite corner – ensuring a one-to-one contact and leaving space between you.

No. 16

Discuss what qualities you would look for in: the perfect hostess – a jet pilot – a nurse – a teacher – a tightrope walker – a policeman – a good car driver.

No. 17. Finding the plausible excuse

Think of some situation where one needs tact and diplomacy. You and your PP take it in turns to be the 'explainer' and the 'explained to'. Grasp the main message; don't worry about individual words.

Suggested situations:

You forgot all about your cousin's birthday until you suddenly ran into her today. Smooth things down.

You have pulled up the prize begonias, thinking they were weeds. Explain.

You are pressed to attend a school sports day. You don't want to go. Give a plausible excuse.

You have no intention of buying your fourteen-year-old daughter a horse. Convince her.

You have, most regrettably, just run over your aunt's favourite cat. How will you deal with the situation, bearing in mind that you have some expectations from aunty?

You have broken the Spode teapot whilst staying with an acquaintance. How do you cope?

Your choice of material is wide.

No. 18. Shared planning of an event

Arranging a children's party.
Designing a garden for a patch 50 feet by 300 feet.
Furnishing a bed-sitting room on £400.
Organizing a sponsored walk.
Running a jumble sale.
Starting a 'Scottish Club' or a 'Welsh Club'.
Having a 'Bring and Buy' coffee morning in aid of a good cause.

No. 19. Proper names

We have already noticed that an unfamiliar proper name is very difficult unless there is a helpful context.

Where there is helpful context and the subject is known, the choice will be within narrower limits. The possibilities and therefore the margin of error will be reduced.

If you know that I have just bought an angora woollie at half price in a sale, it is unlikely that it came from Boots the chemist. It is more likely that it came from Marks & Spencer or from that little boutique round the corner.

A plan is needed to study proper names of both people and places.

No. 19a. Names of people

List the names of people you know and group them under different headings.

1. The people who live in the same house or block of flats as you do.
2. Other neighbours, people you know in the same road; include nearby small shops (Brown's the chemist, Elizabeth's Pantry, Beeney's Hardware etc).
3. Relations – including the nicknames they are known by in the family.
4. People you meet at work or who are connected with your job.
5. People connected with your other activities or interests. This might be at the local golf club, the WI, the church, the Ratepayers Association, trade union, bird-watching club and so on.

Go through each group separately, thinking of two short sentences about each name in the group. In the first sentence use the name near the beginning, and in the second sentence use the name near the end (learn by doing, SAS each sentence, at normal speed of course).

Examples of using list No. 1:

'Mrs Wilberforce lives in the basement flat; she keeps herself to herself.'

'Who do you think was wearing a purple knitted hat with a bobble on top? – Mrs Wilberforce!'

'Mr and Mrs Carpenter live on the ground floor.'

'It's no good calling on Mr and Mrs Carpenter; they're away.'

'Bill and Mary are at flat 3 on the ground floor.'

'Are you free for coffee on Saturday? I'd like you to meet friends of ours downstairs, Bill and Mary.'

'Mr Smithkins lives in the top flat with a magnificent view; he's a bachelor.'

'Coming up in the lift I met Mr Smithkins. He's got an awful cough.'

Go through all the names in this way. You may be surprised how often they crop up in conversation.

Do your best to find out in advance the names of people you are going to meet. Get them written down whenever possible and work at them in your do-it-yourself practice time.

Compare names (always in sentences). Some will be very easy to see, others not so easy. Wilberforce, Winterbottom and Bollingbroke are more easily spotted than Carpenter, Hulme or Carey.

No. 19b (i). Place-names

If you live in a town, start by thinking of the names of different districts. It will be interesting to know something of the history too.

I live in a town of about eighty thousand population. East of the town there is Langney, on flat marshy land, an area developed in the last twenty-five years. At the opposite end, there is 'Old Town', under the hills. It has a very old parish church, St Mary's, and the Lamb Inn opposite is fifteenth century. In between, a long wedge of the town is known as 'Seaside'; between Old Town and the sea is 'The Meads', an expensive locality to live in. An old village, Willingdon, to the north, is now incorporated in the town although it has retained its own individuality. It is mainly residential.

Find out about *your* town. Practice SAS by working out how to get to different parts of the town. For example:

Catch a bus from the Lamb Inn down to Seaside for the shopping precincts. Walk along the sea front from Langney to Meads; it will take you about an hour. The post office in Old Town is in Church Street. The post office in Seaside is in Langney Road. The post office in Meads is in Meads Street.

Think of the location and names of the bus stops, churches and pubs in your own town.

No. 19b (ii)

Think of different towns and counties. What are they noted for?

Melton Mowbray – those delicious meat pies.

Devon – Devonshire cream, cream teas, cider.
Cornwall – Cornish pasties.
Oxford – the city of spires.
Sussex – the Sussex trug basket, still a flourishing industry.
Manchester – rain.
York – ham and, of course, York Minster.
Stoke-on-Trent – pottery and china.
Cheshire – cheese and the Cheshire cat.
Bath and Tunbridge Wells – the waters.
The list is endless. PP may ask, 'What is ... noted for?' or the question may be put the other way round – 'Which city is noted for ...?'

No. 19b (iii)

Plan a journey. You may choose from Cardiff to Bristol; from Coventry to Blackpool; from York to Lindisfarne, or between any other places you fancy. What big towns will you go through? What famous landmarks will you pass?

After you have studied the routes and prepared through do-it-yourself practice, your PP may give the names of the places you pass on one route, and at the conclusion you pick out which of the prepared journeys she was making.

Plan even longer journeys by inter-city train.

No. 19b (iv)

Study the villages in your county – not only their names but a little of their history, the names of houses open to the public, National Trust properties, parks and so on. A little SAS practice can pay dividends (always up-to-time sentences of course).

This subject creates good talking-points.

No. 19c. Other proper names

List flowers in bloom in spring, summer, autumn, winter. After some do-it-yourself study, ask your PP to read one list. You spot what season of the year is appropriate. You may decide to use location instead of season, garden flowers, woodland flowers, flowers that grow on chalk, in the marshes and so on.

It is essential to use normal up-to-time sentences and not exaggerated speech.

No. 20

Use of proverbs provides endless material. Your PP may say a well-known proverb up-to-time and you respond. (If the proverb is not understood first time, the PP writes down the key word and then repeats the whole proverb up-to-time.)

Example: The early bird catches the worm.

Your reply: 'Never be an early worm!'

        or Look before you leap.

Your reply: 'He who hesitates is lost.'

        or There's many a slip 'twixt cup and lip.

Your reply: 'But one swallow doesn't make a summer.'

What proverb uo you think of when the key word is ship, time, apple, gold, friend, cooks?

Unfamiliar proverbs provide advanced practice material. Not only is the subject unknown but the form of words is probably unfamiliar too.

Different nations have their own sayings and proverbs. Why not discover them and weave them into your do-it-yourself material. First you read and memorize a list of ten. Then you use your mirror as you absorb the sound (or memory of sound)/appearance/sensation, always speaking at normal speed, of course.

You may then decide to give a copy of the list to your practice partner and try to spot which one is said when in random order. It will not be so easy to reply instantaneously, so why not number the ten on your list and you can then respond with the number:

Example No. 4 on your list may be the Chinese saying: 'Men grow old – pearls grow yellow – and there's no cure for either.' If this is recognized (the rhythm helps to identify the sentence), then you say, 'No. 4'.

No. 7 on your list may be from Russia: 'The bat cannot see the sun, and so it doesn't believe the sun exists.' You respond by saying, 'No. 7'.

No. 21

One part of a sentence may indicate what the second part is likely to be. For example:

> You won't get an overdraft *unless* you have some security.
> You may miss the train *unless* you go at once.
> I'm going to bed early *because* I've got a headache.
> Please make another pot of tea *because* this one is cold.
> Please stay here *until* I come back.
> Stir the jam *until* it begins to set.

Make a list yourself of sentences which include a 'link' such as: unless
– because – until – therefore – however – so – but – that – if.

No. 22

Very, very small differences can indicate negative or positive
statements. This can be a trap unless the context of the sentence is
revealing.

One morning a husband said to his newly-wed wife, 'Goodbye,
darling. Remember I shan't be in for supper.' She mistook 'shan't' for
'shall' and proceeded to give thought and time to the preparation of a
delicious meal. He returned late that evening to find a very upset and
tearful bride.

If, in the morning, he had said, 'It's a shame I'll be out late this
evening. The meeting doesn't finish until seven, so I shan't be back for
supper', then he would have avoided a painful homecoming and an
upset spouse. Context can come to the rescue.

Compare sentences which indicate a negative or positive by the
helpfulness of context. The following examples are not to be practised
in isolation – only in sentences which indicate the negative or positive:

do	don't
will	won't
can	can't
shall	shan't
should	shouldn't
did	didn't
would	wouldn't
could	couldn't

Think of the upset you may cause by saying, 'I've bought a present for
Barbara. Do/Don't tell her.' Make up two sentences to show if she is
to be told or not – watch them as you say them – hear them in your
mind's ear.

No. 23

A small prefix or suffix is not easily spotted – again the context gives the clue.

Is it *necessary* to fill in the forms in triplicate?
What a lot of *unnecessary* fuss!
There is a *pleasant* view of the river.
There is an *unpleasant* smell from the drains.
The shed has *secure* foundations of concrete.
This ladder is *insecure*. Use the other one.

You will think of many examples, but the differences are so small that context is crucial. SAS the sentences which show the meanings and therefore reveal if it is a positive or negative statement.

No. 24

What do these people wear? An Eskimo – a fisherman – a skin diver – a policeman – a South Sea Islander – a coal-miner – a Red Indian – a nurse – and so on.

Study the list first and then ask your PP to describe what is worn by one group. At first it will be helpful to know which is being described, but later, having worked through the chosen list, you could try to pick out which is being described when one category is chosen (you do not know which) in random order.

The same exercise may be adapted in other ways – for example, where do they live? (In an igloo – a tent – a block of high-rise flats – a farm – and so on.)

No. 25. Happy Families

This exercise and the next continue to give practice in spotting the key word in an up-to-time sentence, in quick thinking and quick response, and in association of ideas. Your PP says: 'What is the name of the offspring when the father is a ... and the mother is a ...?' The dots are filled in with the appropriate names like this:

... when the father is a bull and the mother is a cow.
... when the father is a stallion and the mother is a mare.

It is only the two relevant words which are different every time. The whole sentence is said and you name the 'baby' (which might be a kitten, a puppy, a cygnet, a cub and so on) as quickly as you can. It will help to study the prepared list first.

No. 26

What sort of noise does a ... make?

This exercise depends on only one clue: you know that the clue word is some living creature. Your PP can list the creatures; you then study the list. Your PP reads each sentence up-to-time, and you reply. After going through the list in the known order, be bold and venture to have a go when they are in random order.

Examples:

P.P. What sort of noise does a lion make?

You: It roars.

P.P. What sort of noise does a donkey make?

You: It brays.

You will notice that some creatures have names that are difficult to distinguish from one another (not all are as pleasantly obvious as 'hippopotamus'), which is why it is important for you to read the list first and for the PP to say them in the same order to start with. After five sentences, stop and pause, take a deep breath, look out of the window, then come back to work on the next five sentences.

No. 27 More Happy Families

Winifred Wilberforce was a widow with three children, Sophia, Charlotte and Marmaduke. She married a widower, Jasper Brown, who had three children, George, Barbara and Mary.

PP asks simple questions using their names. For example, what relation was George to Jasper Brown? What relation was George to Marmaduke? What relation was Jasper Brown to Marmaduke Wilberforce? – and so on. The matter is further complicated when Winifred and George have three more children Caroline, William and 'Pudgy'. This involves half-sisters and stepbrothers as well!

No. 28

No set of exercises likely to be used in the British Isles would be complete without some reference to the most talked of subject in the country. Yes. You've guessed! The weather.

You may notice that, whatever anyone says about the weather, it is usual to agree. 'Cold, isn't it?' 'Yes – *isn't* it cold.' 'Lovely morning.' 'Yes – just like spring.' 'Terrible weather, rain, rain, rain.' 'Yes – *isn't* it wet.'

You already know many sayings about the weather. They are stored in your aural memory, excellent for your SAS study sessions.

Rain before seven,
Fine by eleven.

Red sky at night,
Shepherd's delight.
Red sky in the morning,
Shepherd's warning.

He who bathes in May
Will soon be laid in clay.

Cast not a clout
Till May is out.

March comes in like a lion
and goes out like a lamb

The language is rich in weather and country lore. A friend of mine wrote out sixteen well-known sayings in less than fifteen minutes. Can you beat her record?

Finally, a thought to ponder over. When people talk, the sounds they make are nothing like written words. It is the sounds you see/feel/hear in your mind's ear. It is the sounds you interpret.

A child may say, 'Me gwandmuvver's took sick – sawful.' The vicar may hear a hymn in one parish as: 'Prize Him for His grice and fiver' or, in another parish, 'Preeze Him for His grease and fever.'

Part 3

Stumbling-blocks and Stepping-stones

11. Listening Tactics and Social Strategy

Speechreading and social tactics go hand in hand, as much a partnership as strawberries and cream, Marks & Spencer, crumpets and butter.

I have deliberately used the term 'listening tactics' rather than 'hearing tactics' to describe this activity. Listening is subtly different from hearing. Indeed, many people with perfect hearing are poor listeners. Listening demands concentration, a focus of attention; it costs effort, it can be hard work, much harder work when there is a hearing loss.

Listening is harder work in some circumstances than in others. Dealing with fatigue and increasing confidence are all part of listening and social strategies, which is why they have a chapter all to themselves later on.

To say or not to say?

To tell people you are 'deaf' may not result in immediate co-operation. People may shout, mouth words, wave their arms about or feel generally inadequate and give up. Is it sometimes better to avoid the word 'deaf'? To say instead, 'I hear you better if I can see your face' is more positive. It may establish rapport on the right lines – the other person continuing to speak normally.

'I hear you better *when I can see your face*' is a fundamental truth that can be repeated in different ways according to circumstances: 'Please would you repeat that. You spoke when your face was turned away from me' or 'I'll move this vase of flowers so that I can see your face clearly.' Don't be afraid to make your point – go on making it and you will be doing a worthwhile job. Remember, no one will know unless you tell them (and remind them often) that you must see the face of the speaker.

The Sympathetic Hearing Scheme consists of a leaflet for the general public, giving the few simple guidelines, together with a card used by the speechreader. When the card is produced, the speaker is aware that there is a need for co-operation. The symbol is widely used in shops and so on, where a member of the staff is happy to be helpful. Many and varied are the badges available, ranging from 'LIPREADER please speak clearly' in big shiny letters, to a discrete lapel badge showing the sympathetic hearing symbol, to be worn on the reverse of the coat lapel.

Mr T has totally lost his hearing. He never says to a stranger, 'I'm deaf.' He feels it would put him at a disadvantage. Instead he says, 'Please look at me when you talk, because I hear with my eyes.' This is unlikely to get the 'poor-thing-he's deaf' reaction and more likely to get the 'well-how-clever' reaction. It is a positive approach and unlikely to result in the speaker talking in an unnatural way.

So 'to tell or not to tell' is a matter of personal judgement depending on the individual and the circumstances. Both points of view are right if they are right for the person concerned. Not, if I dare say so, if it is an opinion expressed by an onlooker who has not experienced either hearing loss or the unhelpful reactions of the unenlightened.

Lighting

The light should be on the speaker's face, not in your eyes. In your own home, plan accordingly.

The sitting room is the place for sustained conversation. Decide on your favourite chair – back to the window for daytime – always positioned so that you can command a view of all the other people. A central light fitting can be used, but the light that will help you most will be the frontal light reaching your friends' faces from table or standard lamps incorporated in your furnishing scheme.

When you choose a shade for your table or standard lamps, don't choose the thick material that only puts the light up and down. It is the softer, overall light from translucent shades that helps to light faces from the front.

Make it a rule to use good general lighting but to position a standard lamp or table lamp somewhere behind you. Economy in lighting is always false economy. Have several light points and keep a good general level of lighting at all times, using fairly high wattage lamps and switching on early, well before dusk and twilight.

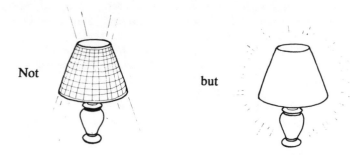

Not   but

Lighting and decoration are complementary. Faces are best seen against a plain background, so avoid heavily patterned wallpaper and fussy wall ornaments. Aim for simple, plain décor and plenty of adequate, well-placed lighting. Wall lighting may result in a face being in unhelpful shadow because seen against the background of a lighted wall.

Speechreading during meals is not easy. Position your dining-room table near to a window and again sit with your back to the light.

When dining in the evening, avoid a single powerful light over the table which will throw an unnatural shadow on everyone's face. If such a light is low over the table, it can leave the diner's face in twilight. Flickering candles may look romantic but can be infuriatingly inadequate for speechreading. Stick to your plan of good general lighting and a standard or table lamp behind you.

In your bedroom, do you keep a dim light glowing gently or the curtains drawn back so that it is never pitch dark? If you happen to open one sleepy eye, can you see the outline of your familiar room and your faithful fluorescent clock? A powerful bedside light is, of course, a must.

Have alternative lighting ready for emergencies: a torch with a battery that *works*, candles, tapers and matches, in a place where they are easily found. On several occasions I have been chatting with someone who relies on speechreading, and suddenly all the lights have gone out, cutting us off completely. While I fumble about, tripping over things, wondering where on earth I last saw a box of matches, my friend wisely sits still and directs me.

Avoid being startled

Having relied for a lifetime on hearing to give information from the environment, it is not easy to replace the instantaneous warning system. It is startling when things and people suddenly appear without being heard, particularly when you believe yourself to be alone in a room.

You may position yourself with your back to the wall, choosing the place giving the best possible view of activities, so that no one will approach from behind.

Animals can 'lend their ears' and be wonderfully understanding. A dog can be a real ally. Fido can be trained to give the alert if someone is at the door, if the telephone is ringing or a visitor is coming up the path. A sensible dog soon learns that barking is not enough and will attract his master's attention in some other way.

With luck, members of the family can also be trained to give warning, for example by flicking the electric light switch when entering the room.

Make full use of mirrors and reflecting surfaces. A mirror on the landing can give a perfect view of the front door although you are upstairs. Where are the mirrors in your house? Are they there for some special purpose or just because there happened to be a nail on the wall for them to hang on? With careful arrangement you can see what is happening in the next room (with an open dividing door or glass panel) or behind you or in the hall, even in the garden, thereby extending your range of vision and your range of information. Reflecting surfaces can be used too: glass on pictures, windows, the TV set. Outside, shop windows, parked cars, even reflections on wet pavements all give extra information.

If you cannot hear water from a running tap, you may not remember to turn it off. A notice at eye level inside the bathroom door can jog your memory and avoid some trying mopping-up operations later.

Now let us go into the kitchen. If you don't hear the milk boiling over, you won't dash to the rescue in the nick of time. Perhaps you already use a 'milk saver', one of those thick glass discs which bounces up and down when the milk boils. The bang as it bounces may be picked up by a hearing-aid or by a vibrator, thus avoiding that sticky mess on top of the stove. The high-pitched kettle may not be audible, but the automatic kettle switches itself off when it boils. The oven with the see-through door and light as well as a timer helps to compensate for the missing sound of your joint sizzling.

You may not hear the 'door porter' through which a visitor announces his name, but you can have a peephole installed in the front door so that you can see the caller before opening the door.

Special environmental aids

Such aids (information from the Royal National Institute for the Deaf) include: a flashing alarm clock or vibrating pillow; fire alarms; various devices for amplifying television (some portable); the baby/invalid alarm; loud or visual doorbells; a telephone with many different call devices (amplified and visual) and different forms of amplification of speech.

The telephone watch receiver is used in two ways: (1) holding it to your other ear when using the 'phone may (depending on your hearing loss) provide better speech reception and prevent interference from background noise; (2) you speak on the telephone in the ordinary way, and someone (a child can do it) listens through the watch receiver and repeats to you what the speaker says, which you then speechread and reply direct to the caller. British Telecom have information on a wide range of equipment to assist hearing impaired people. The supercom enables users with profound hearing loss to enjoy a typed conversation. It is portable, can be used to phone police, car breakdown service, at a public 'phone box (with message to family, office and so on) as well as routine social use. There must be a similar machine at the receiving end.

Teletext not only gives up-to-date news and a wealth of information on different subjects but keeps you informed of sub-titled plays and many special TV programmes which can be followed visually. The improved Palantype has wonderful possibilities.

The loop system, properly installed, can help large numbers of hearing-aid users in public buildings. The loop system should be a matter of routine in all places of worship. Wherever installed there should be a large notice to tell people, regular routine checking to ensure it is in working order, and someone to ensure it is switched on and properly used.

Background noise

Background noise preventing speech reception is a frequent complaint among people whose use a hearing-aid. What can be done?

Obviously remove or reduce the background noise wherever possible. The blaring background TV set can be firmly switched off, the yapping poodle popped into another room, the open window closed so that the traffic noise is shut out, the children given books and lollipops.

Although in theory speechreading should be particularly useful in circumstances where hearing is most difficult, in practice aid-users find that a barrage of distorted sounds can interfere with concentration. This is less disturbing if the hearing-aid is set to a quieter level.

Room acoustics

Room acoustics can completely alter speech reception. We have already noticed that hard wall surfaces, a tiled floor and steel furniture reflect the sounds and increase reverberation. The situation is improved by adding velvet curtains, acoustic tiles and a thick pile carpet.

Look critically at your environment, at your home and place of work and at the halls or rooms where you may have to attend meetings. Often better listening-conditions could be achieved at little cost. You may be the one person to bring about improvements which will benefit many others as well as yourself. Large halls ideal for music can be too reverberant for the spoken word. In a cathedral the choir sounds magnificent, but the unfortunate parson may be inaudible.

If you are attending a meeting, arrive in good time, plan to have a clear view of the speaker, being reasonably close to him with hearing-aid volume low rather than being more distant with the volume at a higher level, picking up more unwanted noise. If a loop system is installed in the room or hall, this will greatly assist the majority of aid-users. If possible, be well informed about the subject beforehand.

It is a mistake to think that only people with hearing loss have difficulty in hearing at meetings. Looking at the audience, you may find that only those in the first five rows are alert and interested – the next five rows are straining forward, probably frowning, while the people in the back of the hall have given up and are doing their best to hide the fact that they are nodding off.

Keep your distance

We have already observed that it is more difficult to speechread unless there is enough space between you and the speaker – eyes cannot possibly focus on the whole face if it is only six inches away. At home you can arrange your seating accordingly, possibly placing some low barrier, such as a coffee table, between you and the speaker. He will be less easy to understand if you literally put your heads together.

Hearing loss at work

Some jobs will be affected more than others. A great deal of thought may be needed to adapt and adjust so that hearing loss causes as little strain as possible. Choice of type of work has usually been made before hearing loss started. If it is absolutely impossible to carry on with one's own job or profession in spite of all possible adjustments and adaptations which can be made, there are two possibilities: (1) to use one's skills and experience through a different channel, or (2) to retrain for something quite different.

Start by assessing the present situation as objectively as possible. Go through a normal working day and write down where the pressures are most difficult. What steps can be taken to make things easier? Would transfer to another department or firm be possible? Explore alternatives – can colleagues be of greater assistance? (For example, is there someone to take your telephone calls?)

Causes of uncertainty are often in the area of giving and receiving instructions and in making sure that information is correctly understood. Use the written word when possible, particularly for factual information of times, prices, dates, sizes and explicit details. You will, of course, study all the written material relating to your work.

Warning and danger signals often depend on hearing. Explore possible alternatives to hooters, whistles, bells and shouts.

It is certainly less strain to be in a job where you relate to and get to know a limited number of people. A sales representative, for example, is not in that position as he meets large numbers of people for a short time. With close colleagues there is more chance of explaining the best way of 'making it easy for them', of getting them on your side as allies.

Different approaches may be needed for a colleague, a partner, an employee. It is probably more difficult to explain to someone who is used to being in a position of authority. One needs tact: to say, 'I hear you better if I see your face' is more promising than telling the boss he mumbles, even if he does! In an executive position a good secretary can greatly ease matters.

Some equipment may be invaluable and will no doubt be reduced in price as demand increases. At present 'Palantype' could be available for a privileged few – it is expensive and requires a full-time operator. Lighting positioning and thought are cheap. I have known a life transformed simply by moving a desk to a more advantageous position.

Committee meetings and discussions

Committee meetings and discussions are an essential part of many jobs. They are extremely difficult with hearing loss. What can be done?

You will pay special attention to preparation, being thoroughly familiar with the matters to be discussed. Study all relevant papers; know the facts. If possible, know your colleagues' views; form your own opinions based on sound facts for which you are able to give convincing reasons in a straightforward manner. Know the subject inside out, putting in that extra effort even if it means reading late and waking early.

At the meeting itself, choose your position with care. Next to the secretary could be a good place, but in any case have a good view of the chairman and of as many colleagues as possible.

Perhaps your secretary or some other intelligent person can sit alongside you and jot down, unobtrusively, the main points made by other speakers and indicate *who* is speaking so that you can look at them and glance at the notes alternately.

An arrangement may be made so that you look at only one person who 'interprets' what is said, through writing or clear speech, but awareness of the 'feel' of the meeting and possible eye contact cannot be easily conveyed at second hand.

It may be difficult for you to make instantaneous response to what is said. However, it is not necessarily the immediate reply which influences decision so much as the well-considered facts succinctly presented. The timing of your own contribution can be planned to be as effective as possible. Your knowledge of the matter in hand will help you to participate. The best-placed person is the chairman of a meeting who is able to direct who should speak (and to stop them!) and therefore knows who is speaking on what subject, and when.

Secretaries of committees often tape-record what is said. Secretaries who have hearing loss may find this particularly useful.

Many employers are impressed by the conscientious service of those who have hearing loss. Alas, this can sometimes cause difficulty with colleagues! The person who gets on with the job instead of wasting time in chatter may show up the less zealous and cause the chatterers to feel vaguely guilty, which of course they won't like. Some firms have personnel officers who can discuss such matters.

Social contact with colleagues outside working times may be restricted – perhaps the background noise in the canteen or the poor lighting conditions at the pub lunch may make conversation near impossible. The business lunch is certainly not easy unless carefully planned first and lighting and positioning chosen.

Obviously you want to avoid appearing 'standoffish' socially, individuals will have very different circumstances to consider.

Retraining, adapting and redirecting skills

Retraining which is academic can be difficult unless some means is provided so that lectures, discussion and talks can be followed. Beware of other people's false expectations that 'all that is needed is lipreading.' Not only is it very tiring, even impossibly exhausting, to rely on speechreading, but where the information may be conveyed in unfamiliar or technical terms, speechreading may not be sufficiently concise for certainty.

When hearing loss is severe, the written word is your main ally, but you may also need the facility of one person who can make sure that you do not miss what is said. There may be a willing volunteer or a professional person specially appointed, but this may not be easy to find. Nevertheless, when this type of assistance is essential to you, the provision should be ruthlessly pursued. The Royal National Institute for the Deaf might advise on sources of provision. The DRO of the Department of Employment, a local hearing therapist or a social worker for the deaf might have useful contacts.

Retraining may not be necessary if new outlets can be discovered for present skills.

A highly qualified horticulturist found his responsible and mainly administrative post terribly exhausting after his hearing became impaired. He went 'back to the land', starting in a small way by looking after other people's gardens and taking a couple of allotments. He first suffered a big financial drop, but when we last met, he was glowing with health and enjoying every minute. His family were enjoying wonderful home-grown vegetables. As I left (clutching a crisp lettuce and firm, shining tomatoes), I thought about his previous job. Possibly it could have led to gastric ulcers and an early coronary, so perhaps the change was a blessing in disguise?

The lecturer in further education found teaching too difficult when his hearing failed. He started to write textbooks – he wrote more and more textbooks – unlike a novel they were in demand from each new intake of students. The last time we met he had just bought a new boat, having taken up sailing in his spare time (but he hasn't much of that).

When a doctor's receptionist suffered a hearing loss, she prepared by carefully noting and practising the names of patients and times of their appointments. She could hear a loud, low-pitched door-bell, always opened the door fully, invited the patient to enter, then left the door open so that the patient turned towards the open door when giving his name. Simply by leaving the door open, the receptionist was sure that the patient's face was in full light whilst speaking.

Incidentally, this enterprising lady took a course in typing and became the practice secretary (she could use an amplified telephone). She was not able to hear well enough to take shorthand, but her pleasant personality and conscientious work made her a valued member of staff. I need to write another book to tell you about some of the astonishing ways in which skills can be redirected. Unexpected opportunities have been discovered and new doors opened.

What matters is assessing situations which are possible and those that, even with thought and adaptation, are not possible, and using the possibilities to full advantage.

Travel

Again, be prepared. Study the route first when going by train; check the time at which you should arrive at various stations and the time of arrival at destination. Start off with time in hand so that you can read notices and indicators in a calm state of mind; buy your ticket in advance; know exactly when you have to change and the time of the connections. (Will there be time for coffee before Crewe? Should you get your luggage down as the express hurls itself through Lower Poppleton?) Take a timetable with you and pore over it. If possible, avoid travel in the rush hour.

'A deaf driver is a safe driver.' There is much evidence that this is true. A driver with impaired hearing is observant and undistracted by chatting passengers, exciting radio programmes and back-seat drivers. Explain to your passengers before you start that your eyes and your concentration must be on the road. In emergency the person in the seat next to you may be allowed to indicate 'slow down' by moving his straight right arm gently up and down in front of him (*not* in front of you!); then you will find a place to pull in and stop. Only then will he say what he has to say. If it is simply 'Look at those jolly rabbits' – well, bad luck – he is half a mile too late. However, if it is 'Look out for the Purple Pig on your right in half a mile so that we can pull in for lunch', then this is more reasonable.

As a speechreading passenger, it is an easy matter to arrange a mirror on the visor so that you can see the passenger in front and chat in the ordinary way. The driver may also arrange a mirror additional to the driving mirror so that the speechreading passenger sitting next to him sees his face. Naturally a good driver will not turn his head to talk to his companion.

Aeroplane travel is just about the easiest. At 'check-in', mention that you won't hear the flight number called. The receptionist then writes clearly, 'You will be told when it is announced', and as if by magic one of those charming, immaculate stewardesses will make sure that you do know. Of course the visual indicators are useful but not so personal or so reassuring (or so charming), and you cannot talk to them about delays and 'Are there free sandwiches and coffee?' However, as one speechreader said to me, 'By using my eyes, I often find my way around large terminals and airports much more easily than my friends who can hear and who are automatically inclined to rely on announcements.'

Travelling by bus in a strange place, have small change ready. The conductor or a friendly passenger may tell you where to alight. You will notice names of towns on signposts, post offices and so on. You may find out before the journey a particular landmark near your destination. Some bad moments may arise paying fares on buses. If the fare should be around 20-30p, give 50p. Count your change and remember the fare for next time.

Shopping

Supermarket prices are clearly marked, and the total can be seen on the cash register. If there is uncertainty and the operator is looking down when saying the totals, it may be useful to make no move. The operator will then look up, puzzled, and see your friendly face as you ask her to repeat the amount. The friendly smile works wonders.

Your village or corner shop, on the other hand, usually gives the opportunity for a friendly chat. This in itself is worth paying a penny or two more on sultanas, and it provides regular contact with the shopkeeper, who will soon realize that 'you hear her better if you see her face'.

Banks, post offices, ticket offices and other places may have glass or a grille between you and the speaker. Behind the grille it is usually quieter than outside (where you are), and the muffled voice may have to compete with loud background noise; in addition the speaker's face often cannot be seen clearly. Certainly not a situation in which to ask important questions. Some rail ticket offices have a written form available, some banks and railway booking offices have loop systems installed, ideal for most hearing aid users, who can then just switch to the T position.

In every situation, aim to plan ahead. When visiting the house agent, bank, garage or pet shop or making plans for the wedding reception and so on, go through the events mentally first. Think of the likely replies to your question; think of the vocabulary you will meet. Weave it into your do-it-yourself practice. Do all you can to prepare, then go forward to meet the occasion with confidence.

Family life

All members of the family are bound to be affected if father or mother suffers a severe hearing loss. A partner may feel cut off from their spouse unless they know how to communicate easily. By being able to recognize and share mutual difficulties, they can be tackled in partnership.

Meal-time is usually a family get-together, where the doings of the day are talked about. The little things, silly jokes, family news, plans and questions are significant to the whole family. Speechreading needs that bit of extra consideration from others.

If two of the family are chatting about something special, perhaps they could do it another time or alternatively make absolutely sure that you know what it is all about. You should still play a full part in the family, the discussions and decision-making.

Arrange definite times and a workable routine. If father is the speechreader, he should regularly spend that little extra time with the children. He is the one to tell the bedtime stories, to chat and play games with the children, specially to have this contact when children are small (the ride-a-cock-horse, the 'carry round' shoulder high, the five little piggies, the boats in the bath).

People with families, sometimes where both partners are working, are very busy people, often talking to each other only when doing a hundred and one other things too. Now, with hearing loss, the routine needs to be reviewed, to plan when to talk and when not to. Having arrived home at the end of a working day, tired and hungry, this is not the best moment to concentrate on conversation. After a meal, when relaxing over a cup of coffee, it is easier to discuss important matters – even a crisis can usually wait for an hour or so before being thought about and tackled.

Half an hour together regularly and uninterrupted every evening is tremendously helpful to some couples. Your special time for catching up together cannot be shared with exuberant teenagers, the unexpected caller or a visiting relative. It is in your special half-hour that you can consult and plan, discuss opinions, ask advice, make decisions. Make it a firm arrangement faithfully followed, and do not allow all the other urgent distractions to crush out this opportunity.

A place you may agree not to talk in is in the kitchen. If attention and eyes are on the washing-up, it is unwise to try to speechread as well and frustrating to stop in the middle to look at the speaker (possibly expensive in breakages too!) Hearing-aids pick up the clatter of dishes and swoosh of running water, which compete with speech reception. The kitchen is a workplace in its own right; there is a job to be done, and it will be impossible for the speechreader to deal with the matter in hand if eyes have to be constantly switched to the speaker's face. It is most annoying to have unintelligible chattering somewhere behind you whilst watching the fish or beating the eggs.

Social events and entertaining

These often present a challenge that is hidden to everyone but you!

Small, informal groups of people are likely to chatter away nineteen-to-the-dozen. Weigh up the pros and cons; decide if it is better to accept such invitations or to spend the time doing your own thing, perhaps sharing a mutual interest with one friend.

The key to social satisfaction is in meeting like-minded people with a mutual interest – whether or not they happen to have a hearing loss is incidental. Only very superficially does it appear to be significant. This, of course, is not the same for people born deaf, who may share the same educational background and cultural experience. It is the common bond of a mutual interest or kindred spirit which is satisfying.

When with a group, is it better to laugh or not to laugh at the joke you don't hear? Is it dishonest to laugh? Surely there can be no firm rule: everything depends on the company. With your close family and real friends, there is no need for deception. However, if you are with a group and everyone is laughing, it might put a damper on things if you remained tight-lipped and poker-faced. There is no deception in a smile, in looking pleasantly relaxed.

Doubtless you will agree that Mrs McG took things too far: whenever the speaker's mouth went up, she said, 'Yes, yes,' and whenever the mouth went down, she said, 'What a pity!' There was no real communication, although surprisingly few people were aware of the fact.

Perhaps one of the worst moments in a group is described by H.K.B., an excellent speechreader.

> When you are with a group of people and someone decides to be kind and 'bring you in', out of the blue you will be told 'We are talking about ...' which could be anything ranging from the Prime Minister's latest speech or last night's TV programme to the odd behaviour of the woman next door. At this point you have got to say something interesting or else the conversation will pass on and leave you isolated once more. Grab your chance: explain what it is like to be confronted with a subject without any preparation. You might try it on them, almost like a competition. Not only does this help people to understand the problems of deafness, but it often produces a lot of fun.

When entertaining, much depends on the kind of entertainment you like, and what adaptations may be possible so that it is still a pleasure and not a strain.

Invite one person – perhaps to a meal (you have prepared first) – and you have an opportunity of a pleasant evening of conversation in your own home. If husband and wife are entertaining, then invite another couple. The partner of the speechreader will take special care that the conversation remains 'one-to-one' and not three people talking together, which leaves the speechreader on a solitary island.

Going to other people's parties is not easy and often noisy for the aid-user. Arranging your own party is the answer. You know all the guests and something about them; you can greet, welcome, introduce and generally make them feel at home. If you invite only three or four, the conversation may become general, and you are likely to be left out, so be bold: invite twenty people, then you can move around, making contact with individuals as you ply them with food and drink, or sit with one person for a short chat before moving on to another.

A formal dinner means that the person opposite you is probably the only one well placed for speech readability; those on either side of you are too close. On formal occasions there may be a speaker or two: once seated, you are not able to change your position to get a better view, so, if possible, choose your seat first. A buffet meal is much easier and more sociable, enabling you to circulate freely.

Questions – closed or open

It is always easier to understand the answers to your own questions because you know the subject and, within limits, can anticipate likely or possible replies. How can the element of chance be reduced even further? Much depends on how the question is formulated so that the answer is yes or no. Of course the yes or no may be qualified by various trimmings, for example: 'Do you drive?' The reply could be: 'Yes, when my husband isn't using the car' or 'Yes, I go into the village on Mondays' or 'No, but I'm taking my test next week' or 'No. I used to but I've given up since my accident.'

If the question is framed to give a yes or no reply, it is a 'closed' question. The area of doubt is reduced. An 'open' question produces a reply which leaves more room for uncertainty.

An example of an open question is: 'What did you do on Saturday afternoon?' The reply cannot be anticipated – it could be: 'Played golf,' 'Visited mother,' 'Planted the carrots' or even 'Searched for haddock's eyes among the heather bright.' A closed question is: 'Did you play golf on Saturday?' and (hopefully) you get a yes/no answer, probably with a few embellishments. To clarify information, frame your question to cut out alternatives.

When seeking information, use a closed question for a yes/no answer. Give the person all the information needed in order to reply. For example: 'May I have an appointment with Mr Block at 4 p.m. on Monday next for a short back and sides?' is preferable to: 'I want an appointment please,' which leads to a string of questions, 'Which day?' 'What for?' 'Who with?' 'What time?'

If there is uncertainty about a number – for example, was it fourteen or forty? – think which is more likely. If it is more likely to be fourteen, ask: 'Did you say one-four?' The reply should come back as yes/no. However, if you merely ask for a repetition of the number, it still may not be clear if it is fourteen or forty. They look very similar anyway.

A prescription for coping with deafness

A prescription for 'coping with sudden severe hearing loss' by Dr Colin Green:

   A lot of motivation

A touch of inspiration
As much as possible of guidance
Hopefully, a lot of resilience
Mixed with some dedication
Flavoured with faith
Coloured with a sense of humour
All mixed together with ... a little bit of luck.

12. Dealing with Stressful Tension and Fatigue

Stressful tension and fatigue directly affect speechreading ability. Tension and fatigue are two different things, but both can be relieved, even controlled, by relaxation.

In my experience the affect of stressful tension and fatigue is rarely recognized by speechreaders and those he meets, and yet it is the enemy of effective communication even when hearing is perfect.

There are many different causes of stressful tension: worry, fear, uncertainty, nervousness, anxiety and so on.

The medical profession increasingly recognize stressful tension as the underlying cause of many illnesses, a cause of much discomfort and widespread unhappiness to many people whether or not they hear well. Of course, not all tension is stressful. Nervousness can be of different kinds, and a certain excitement and exhilaration may actually increase awareness and stimulate ability.

Because you are observant, you will notice that some people, when on their own, look serene and content but others certainly do not.

Look at solitary drivers waiting in a traffic jam. That driver of the Rover (with a dog in the back seat) is looking calm – sitting back – almost smiling – perhaps actually enjoying the enforced pause. However, behind the wheel of the Audi there is a different picture. The driver is sitting forward, biting his lip and frowning, revving the engine, shifting, drumming his fingers; impatience and annoyance are being expressed through every pore of his being. One driver will arrive at the destination ready to deal with the next thing, the other will be on edge, probably snappy and even with dangerously raised blood pressure. Both drivers were subjected to irritation but their responses were different. The driver of the Audi allowed the circumstances to upset him, but his feelings of annoyance did not alter the traffic jam in the slightest.

I wonder if this can tell us anything useful about meeting situations which may cause stressful tension? It certainly illustrates the point that there is a close relationship between mind and body. The resented traffic jam, the heated political argument, the broken appointment, can cause strong feelings of resentment, exasperation and frustration which have a physical effect.

Stressful tension is not always apparent to the person suffering from it, but unless it is released it can build up until physical symptoms are felt: some of these may take the form of headaches, of 'butterflies in the tummy', of rapid heart beats, of a feeling of pain at the back of the neck, poor sleeping, poor digestion, a pain like a sharp knife on the left side of the breastbone, shallow breathing, a tightness in the throat which can become quite painful. These may not be recognized as symptoms of stress – that is, until the stress is reduced and the symptoms disappear.

Unless the stressful tension is released, it will not improve the health, the temper or the situation. It can be released through physical action such as sawing logs, by stamping one's foot onto the accelerator and driving like a maniac or simply by smashing a plate. However, there are better and easier methods, which we will discuss later.

Why is stressful tension significant to speechreaders?

Hearing loss often increases the circumstances which can cause stressful tension. This, together with fatigue, can prevent progress. Tinnitus may be an added cause of stress.

Causes of worry, anxiety and fear have their roots in uncertainty. Speechreading is an uncertain art; successful speechreading depends on more than the skill of the individual: it also depends on the circumstances and the speaker.

Hearing loss can cause painful misunderstandings and can be extremely exasperating; tempers may become frayed, and stressful tension may be allowed to mount. Communication will not be improved.

Stressful tension can cause a 'panic block'. A speechreader may be on top form and have no problems in understanding unimportant asides or trivial chatter, but at the vital interview panic sets in. Almost like a rabbit looking at a snake, the mind is in a vice of non-comprehension. Yes, the speaker's lips are moving, but somehow the sense does not come through the 'panic block'.

Paradoxically, being over-anxious has caused a barrier. Concentration is no longer on the message the speaker is conveying but, instead, the importance of the occasion; there is conscious striving to understand. The subconscious mind works best when allowed to get on with its own job. The stressful tension must be dealt with firmly and decisively.

Fatigue is increased by the constant effort required to be an active listener. The alert, attentive mind, the intense concentration needed, is very demanding.

When people begin speechreading instruction, their eagerness to progress and to understand everything instantly makes them very vulnerable to fatigue. They may strain forward with muscles tense, hands gripped until the knuckles show white through the skin, and eyes staring unblinkingly. It is not easy to accept that, like a plant that grows, the process may be gradual (although sometimes this is not the case). Little and often, with relaxed pauses between, achieves more than long periods occasionally.

It is easier to speechread when you are in good health, on top of your form, when you are not tired. It is easier when you are feeling fresh and alert after a good night's sleep than at the end of a busy day, easier for short periods than for long periods.

Stress and fatigue can create a vicious circle. Because of fatigue you may understand less well; comprehending less well, you strain harder to understand; this extra effort increases fatigue and so on.

Signs of stressful tension

Some of the signs of tension: strained face, tight jaw, hunched shoulders, sitting on the edge of the chair, holding breath, fidgeting and 'fiddling', clenched hands, restless movements (tapping, foot, drumming fingers). Check yourself, this minute. Are you reading with a frown on your face? If so, stop, take your eyes off the book, take a deep breath, allow your face muscles to relax and then come back to read the next sentence with even keener interest but with less strain.

In order to tackle the problem let us think of short-term and long-term strategy.

Tackling the problem: short-term strategy

1. *Learn to listen actively but with ease.* Allow the sense to come to you, using the threefold strands of sound (or memory of sound)/appearance/sensation. Your mind will be attentive, aware but unflurried. Allow your eyes to observe in an easy, natural way but not to stare unblinkingly as if to bore holes in whatever or whoever they are looking at. Learn to pay attention without stressful tension. Allow things to happen – do not strive anxiously.

This may seem a paradox and different from the usual pattern of learning, therefore it needs to become a habit. Check yourself frequently for signs of stressful tension.

2. *A fifteen-second refresher* gives you that vital pause which will enable you to speechread for longer stretches at a time than would be possible otherwise. There are four steps.

    a. Stop. Check yourself for signs of physical tension (as listed previously). Let go the tension spot. If shoulders are up, let them drop; if jaw is clenched, allow your teeth to part, and so on.

    b. At the same time, shift your position slightly.

    c. Also take a deep breath – letting it out in a puff.

    d. At the same time, blink once or twice, change eye focus, look into the distance – perhaps out of the window – then look down to the floor.

This very short break will enable you to return to speechreading with renewed energy, impetus and enthusiasm.

The fifteen-second restorer need not be obvious to other people. There are many ways in which their attention can be distracted – 'Would you care to glance at these estimates?' 'Be a dear and put out the cat', 'This train timetable may help you' and so on. Choose your opportunity. Short breaks in concentration help you to sustain much longer conversations.

3. *Temporary relief from worry and anxiety* can be achieved by totally occupying the mind with something else. A hobby that demands complete attention is refreshing because it is totally absorbing.

Write your worry down clearly and firmly, then go off and do something else, leaving the worry there on paper all ready for you when you return. When you look at it next time, solutions may suggest themselves, and it can be looked at more objectively. You have already defined what the worry is, so go on to look at the cause, list different possibilities for dealing with the cause and then decide on the action which seems most likely to be effective. Transfer attention away from your own anxiety: 'Turn your mirrors into windows.'

Tackling the problem: long-term strategy

Your long-term strategy will need thinking through according to your own circumstances.

Periods of concentration and relaxation should balance and complement each other. This achieves much more in the long run than attempting to concentrate for a long time until fatigue sets in. Aim to have frequent breaks *before* becoming overtired.

Coping with hearing loss takes a great deal of energy. For everyone energy is limited, a precious commodity. It can be squandered by the litre but only returns drop by drop. Fear, worry, anxiety and stressful tension absorb precious energy which would be more usefully channelled into constructive directions.

You may like to plan your long-term strategy under three approximate headings of: mental/physical serenity and poise; relaxation; planned participation.

An alert, calm state of mind which remains unruffled may already be one of your assets. If not, it is worth acquiring: it aids speechreading, and it is helped by taking stock realistically, by advanced preparation and by self-confidence.

List the particular circumstances which cause frustration and stressful tension to mount. Are there ways in which you can avoid or alter these circumstances? What a challenge to transform and use them as an asset!

If no alternative can be found, then remember the driver of the Rover in the traffic jam. Find out ways to tolerate the apparently unchangeable circumstance; to live through it without becoming upset or ruffled, remind yourself that it won't last forever. When you cannot alter or control difficult circumstances, you can control how much you allow them to affect you.

'As a man thinks – so he is' – a statement that has proved itself down the years. A searching question is, 'What are you really seeking?' Once that is decided, the unimportant trifles are put firmly in their place, not worth worrying about, not worth the attention they clamour for.

Correct use of the body – ergodynamics

The correct use of the body influences one's outlook and general happiness. Ease of movement and energy wisely directed help to untie the physical knots which stressful tension can all too easily create.

Even very simple things such as the correct height of tables, chairs, desks and working-surfaces can increase effectiveness and conserve precious energy.

The study of such commonsense matters goes under the delightful name of ergodynamics. (Why not add it to your do-it-yourself mirror practice? 'Please give my apologies – tonight I am studying applied ergodynamics.;)

The following story shows how a small adjustment can make a big difference.

Saving energy – and backache

Some energy-savers through correct posture[14]

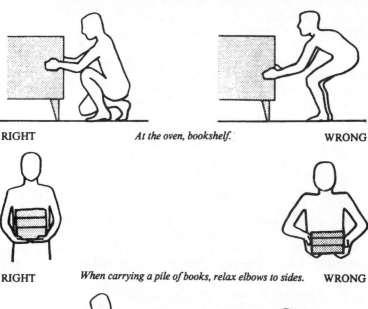

RIGHT   *At the oven, bookshelf.*   WRONG

RIGHT   *When carrying a pile of books, relax elbows to sides.*   WRONG

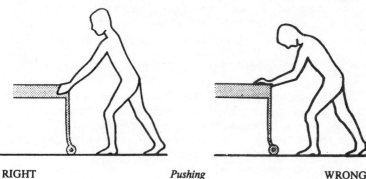

RIGHT   *Pushing*   WRONG

Miss X wrote children's books. She developed uncomfortable neuritis in her right shoulder: 'writer's cramp' she decided with resignation and bought herself a typewriter. Unfortunately she never bothered to learn to touch-type but used instead the 'poke and dig' method. This can produce bad posture and always involves using the eyes. Her books were produced more slowly and with much frustration. Eventually she gave up and decided to keep pigs instead.

What a pity she did not discover that all she needed in the first place to remove the 'writer's cramp' was to rest her right elbow on the table when writing instead of letting it hang over the edge without support! The discovery could have altered her life.

Movements and posture used daily when doing different jobs or in different occupations can save or squander energy. Aches and pains, backache, headache and general feeling of vague discomfort can be caused by using the body in a way it doesn't like. How do you walk, move, sit, stand?

Here is a little verse taken from the *Reader's Digest*:

In walking by a mirror fast
I vaguely wondered whom I passed.
I backed up several steps to see
And – what a shock! The shock was me!

Notice posture. Watch people walking. Some shuffle and bustle along, with stiff, tense movements, head poking forward. How different from the rhythmic swing of the person who enjoys walking, the straight back and head held high. When carrying shopping-baskets and holdalls, take care that the weight is evenly distributed. If all the weight is on one side and being lugged along, it will upset the natural poise and balance of the body. It will use more energy, be more tiring.

Concentration and relaxation

Concentration and relaxation are complementary. Keep the balance; realize that relaxation is an essential part of your long-term plan.

Have faith in your subconscious mind and the benefit of rest and recreation. Learn how to save energy by minimizing unnecessary actions and using essential ones in the correct way.

Aids to relaxation include:
deep, slow breathing to the bottom of the lungs –
(breathe out before you begin) –
drop shoulders; allow jaw to drop –
support arms and head on cushions –
sit well back in chair, thighs supported –
slow, circular shoulder movements –
massage neck, scalp and shoulders –
rhythmic walks in fresh air, allowing arms to swing easily –
good posture when standing; thinking tall.
It is difficult to persuade overworkers of the importance of rest and

recreation. It is difficult to persuade people who are eagerly straining to learn to speechread that it is also important to learn how to stop.

Redirect the stressful tension or release it, and you increase your ability. Plan your periods of relaxation; relax in spare moments before you get tired.

Suggested reading

In an age of increasing stressful tension and uncertainty, people search (sometimes desperately) in different ways and different places for solutions – tranquillizers, yoga, alcohol and so on. Libraries have shelves full of books, and books have pages of 'methods'. The following books on different aspects of dealing with stressful tension may give you new ideas.

The New Way to Relax by Karin Roon (Cedar paperback No. 35), is about causes of tension and aids to physical relaxation.

Choice of Habit, by Jack Vinten Fenton (MacDonald and Evans Ltd), is about ergodynamics, with telling illustrations (one is shown on page 149).

Silent Music, by William Johnson (paperback, Fontana Collins), is about the science of meditation.

Books by Carlo Carletto, Archbishop Anthony Bloom, Archimandrite Sophromy (Collins; Darton Longman & Todd; Mowbrays respectively) are about prayer.

The Prophet, by Kahlil Gibran (ideal rhythmic sentences for SAS practice, this one – published by Heinemann), is philosophical.

Any books on the Alexander Method co-ordinate thinking and doing in a creative way.

A practical exercise

Before we leave the subject, try the following practical relaxation exercise:

1. Lock your door, set whatever device will rouse you at a definite time (cooking-timer, flashing alarm clock, vibrator) – set it to go off in eight minutes.

2. Lie on the floor on your back (on the carpet, of course, not on cold concrete or lino). You may need a thin book under your head if it drops back uncomfortably.

3. Allow yourself to uncurl so that arms and legs are at rest, not curled up.

4. Let your tongue rest, allow your face and jaw muscles to ease – probably into a 'near smile'.

5. Shut your eyes. Feel the floor taking your whole weight. Feel that your quiet, heavy limbs are almost spreading out and sinking into the floor like water that has been spilled.

6. Allow yourself to breathe easily, gently and deeply. Remind yourself that everything else can wait. There is nothing to do but do nothing.

7. When your reminder device goes off, don't hurry. Don't stop relaxing and leap up. Instead, stretch, curl up and slowly reach sitting position by pressing the palm of your hands on the floor, keeping your chin down, touching your throat. Once sitting (it will be sideways because the palms of your hands are on the floor), slowly raise your head. Stop there for a moment or two before standing up. The gradual return to the vertical may take two minutes. So you have spent ten minutes in all. (The world has just had to manage without you!)

8. Remind yourself that relaxation costs nothing but can pay dividends in better health and in better speechreading. Unlock your door. Cope confidently and calmly with whatever is waiting on the other side of it.

Planned participation

A person with impaired hearing has to take a lot more strain than people with normal hearing. It should be recognized and accepted that coping with hearing loss can be utterly exhausting.

Do not continue to meet and talk with people non-stop all the time. Plan periods when there is no need to be with anyone and when there is an opportunity to relax and to recharge energy.

Any recreation which means continually trying to understand other people (for example, the small group when the conversation rushes about like a squashball) is very far from recreation. It is likely to be a depressing experience if one is already tired after a day's work and possibly even more frustrating with background noise and dim lights.

Consider carefully which invitations to accept. If they will overload your 'listening' capacity, it may be better to refuse tactfully but firmly. Study your daily programme. If you are meeting people in the morning and a lot of talking is involved, try to have a complete break (without having to speechread) before you tackle the afternoon. If you know you will be with people in the evening too, it would be ideal to have the afternoon away from people altogether or to postpone the evening appointment. Fit in periods away from people, giving yourself the opportunity to renew your energy and rest your eyes. Then return refreshed with added zest and sparkle to participate in the particular circumstances which you have prepared for and chosen.

Final thoughts

Is it possible to become too intense, over-anxious, too deadly earnest? Can you plan one afternoon a week just to enjoy yourself? Don't try to become good at speechreading or at anything else. Unwind, have a good laugh, stuff this volume under a cushion, brew your most expensive coffee and have it with cream. Be a little bit extravagant. It is a worthwhile investment in a very good cause.

Finally, some quotations to reflect upon:

A man is what he thinks about all day long. (Emerson)

When Fate hands us a lemon, let us try to make lemonade. (Dale Carnegie)

Faith is one of the forces by which men live, and the total absence of it means collapse. (William James)

God grant me the serenity to accept the things which cannot be changed, the courage to change those that should be changed, and the wisdom to know the difference. (Anon)

Change your outlook and you change your world.

13. From Fear to Confidence

Confidence is crucial. Confidence is catching. Can confidence be cultivated?

Confidence helps to create good communication. Lack of confidence can destroy it.

Calm confidence is one of the most valuable ingredients in the speechreader's equipment. Why is it that hearing loss can play havoc with self-confidence? Here are some reasons:

Mishearing can cause misunderstandings which may be embarrassing or even funny but certainly not reassuring. Mistakes are bound to happen sometimes. Regard them as an annoying incident, a mere ripple on the pool – do not drown in it, it is not the end of the world. In spite of mistakes there will be many successes.

Othere people's reaction to hearing loss may be less than encouraging, particularly when they are unimaginative and unable to grasp the true facts.

Your own ability will vary. You will have off days when you are tired or a bit under the weather.

You are bound to meet some people and some situations which preclude speechreading. It is unfortunate, but it is not your fault.

It is all too easy to become discouraged, particularly if you are in an atmosphere of indifference or with people who lack insight.

Learning how to survive unhelpful influences and attitudes is part of living. Your 'defence mechanisms' may need to be reviewed, polished and strengthened.

Self-confidence is not a childish show of bluster or conceit (similar to that of Toad of Toad Hall) but is based on a quiet serenity founded on your own self-image. Your deafness is not *you*. Remember, and keep remembering, that you are special because you are a person, not because you do (or don't do) a particular job or because of what you do (or don't) possess.

You, as a person, matter. No one else in the world has had your experience of life, sees the world through your eyes or treads the same path through life 'towards the light of your particular guiding star' (this is described in a rather dull way as 'motivation').

You matter not because you are better or worse than other people but because you are different from them. You are unique. Therefore, you have something very special to contribute to the sum of things.

There may be times when you need to remind yourself of this fact. For example, if there are difficult occasions when everyone seems to be chatting happily and you are left in a limbo of social redundancy. Drawing on your reserve of quiet self-confidence, you may change this painful situation of total frustration into being an interested observer, learning all you can, using the opportunity to be aware of people and their reactions to each other, using the practice material there in front of your nose and being content to wait until you have decided if you wish to participate and have considered how to create the opportunity.

Protecting your self-confidence

Remember that you are not alone in experiencing discouragement. You may meet those who are themselves unhappy, bitter, cynical, twisted and limited, who are likely to express these feelings in a destructive way, particularly in their attitudes towards others. Being disenchanted with life, they may resent those who are contentedly coping with things as best they can and are making a good job of it. Sometimes their discouragement is deliberate and malicious, as happened with Miss K.

Miss K is doing a magnificent, demanding and difficult job, nursing her courageous mother, who is badly disabled. They have a wonderfully happy relationship. An acquaintance met Miss K: 'You look tired,' she said. 'Well we didn't get much sleep last night, so I am a bit tired,' replied Miss K. 'Good,' replied her acquaintance. 'Your damned cheerfulness has always annoyed me.' Well, that was at least honest!

Some people are entirely unaware of their effect. They might be shocked if they realized their destructive influence on those they meet. Last night I was at a social gathering. Mrs P came up to my friend. 'My dear,' she said, 'I haven't seen you for years. You *are* wearing well, grey hairs and all,' and then she poodled off. My friend and I smiled at each other.

Beware of adverse suggestions! Sometimes a sympathetic friend can be a constant source of discouragement, all unknowingly. Discouragement may be given in small doses, but the cumulative effect, like dripping water, leaves its mark.

'My dear, you must feel absolutely awful. Of course you won't be able to cope tomorrow. If I were you, I should put off that interview until next week. You should have an early night, but I don't suppose you will sleep. I know you just feel you can't face tomorrow. Of course you feel very depressed. You can't fool me. You *are* depressed aren't you?'

By that time you are! Make a note to strengthen your defences against future encounters, speculate on the likely result of introducing your 'sympathetic' friend to Mrs P, then make yourself a cup of tea.

Sometimes destruction of self-confidence is given in one fatal dose, enough to kill all enterprise unless you are able to let it bounce off you.

Great achievements require confidence and always meet with criticism, often with derision. If such discouragement had been heeded, penicillin would never have been discovered, Florence Nightingale would have stayed home with her tatting and Hannibal would not have attempted to take elephants across the Alps.

Confidence is catching

In speechreading confidence can be the key factor.

Moods and feelings are infectious. Have you noticed the effect of a genuine smile of welcome, how it can put a stranger at ease? If you are in an anxious state of mind and feeling self-conscious, the other person may feel vaguely uneasy. If you think not of yourself and your own feelings but of the other person, your interest and concern is likely to evoke a response.

Many people are shy, nervous, insecure. *You* can put them at ease. *Your* genuine interest will reassure them.

If someone realizes you do not hear well, perhaps they are wondering if they will be understood and perhaps they feel unsure what to do. They need the encouragement and reassurance you can give, being at ease yourself.

It is always a mistake to fight nervousness. Allow your mood to be one of confidence, forget about yourself, think of the other person. In promoting an easy social atmosphere, rest on your own self-confidence which is soundly based. This attitude protects you from negative suggestions and strengthens your defence mechanism in a socially acceptable way.

This does not mean 'assertive behaviour' that ignores the feelings of other people but rather the recognition that they, too, are unique and special.

Protection from the inquisitive

You may meet the inquisitive or those who try to invade your privacy. This can be kindly meant, but your hearing loss must not mean that you discuss matters that you would prefer not to discuss, solely because it gives an opportunity for conversation.

Albert Schweitzer pointed out that there is a modesty of spirit which should not be violated, although occasionally one's close friends may be revealed to one in special moments, almost like a flash of lightning which illuminates briefly but clearly. Today, respect for this inner sanctum of the spirit is not particularly fashionable.

You probably know instinctively if those whom you meet are genuinely interested or if they are inquisitive, curious, trying to manipulate or probe. Here is an example of what I mean.

Mrs A: I'm sure you won't mind my asking, but how old are you?
Miss B: (Thinks, 'Inquisitive old so-and-so' – but says with charming smile:) Of course I don't mind, but that's something I don't discuss.
Mrs A: (a little aggrieved) I don't mind telling *you* how old *I* am.
Miss B: Now isn't that interesting. Do have another helping of trifle. I'm afraid there's no sherry in it.

Or perhaps Mrs A is holding forth on her views on battered wives or battery hens or baptizing babies, really with the hope of having a head-on argument or of converting someone to her way of thinking. Miss B may not want this. 'Well, well,' she says (charmingly), 'you do have such an interesting point of view – by the way, did I show you the begonias? Only a modest show this year because of the mice.' With luck the conversation is defused into either mice or begonias, and then you will get a chance to get a word in edgeways rather than listen to a lecture which could become controversial or boring (and hard work to speechread).

Knowing you look right

Confidence is strengthened by knowing that you look right. The first impression people receive will be of your appearance. No one would claim that appearance is everything, but it is true that appearance reveals much about us.

Sidle into a room apologetically, look a hopeless failure and people may assume that you are. Look your best, take that little bit of extra care (it's not only what you wear but how you wear it), look at the world squarely and confidently, and other people will expect something good. These positive expectations will help you even before you start talking.

Clothes need not be expensive to be becoming. A choice of colour or new hairdo, lipstick that only a fashion model would wear, could work wonders for a woman. I feel most comfortable in a special dress which is just the right shade and style. Every bride looks beautiful – this is partly because of what she is wearing and partly because she is usually glowing with happiness. It has nothing at all to do with 'being pretty'. A perfectly fitting suit or a daring tie could give a man that added something, revealing the competence which he knows in his heart he has already.

The outer layer – what we look like – can work for us in another way too. What we look like may be what we are gradually becoming.

Think of a young, impressionable person who is on the edge of some fringe set – perhaps eager to be accepted, although doubtful of all the ideas and implications involved. Once his appearance has been changed to identify him with the group (it may be dyeing his hair shocking pink or wearing a big badge), then not only will other people assume that he has agreed to all the ideas and implications of the movement but he himself will be more likely to feel this to be true, even to throw all doubt to the four winds without further investigation.

There are many images created by appearance: the policeman's blue uniform and deliberate pace; the gown and wig of the barrister; the white coat of the hospital workers. I still remember my surprise at the changed attitudes I noticed in other people when I first put on a white coat. I wanted to say, 'But I'm still *me*.'

If what we look like can influence how we feel about ourselves and influence other people's attitudes, then let us cash in on it by taking an interest in appearance. The mental effect of suddenly sitting up straight, squaring your shoulders, breathing deeply, can make you look and feel like a person who can change the world. If you believe it, everyone around you can believe it too.

Beware of the 'poor me' and 'stupid me' image

Check what you say about yourself to other people. Avoid negative comments.

Many people constantly tell everyone how bad they are at almost everything. 'Of course I've never been able to cook. I can't cope at all without a tin-opener – I'm really hopeless – and of course it's too late to start at my age. I can hardly boil an egg.' Alas! This may be only too true, but if so, why advertise the fact? Does the speaker really want to be known as 'poor Nell, such an incompetent twit'. Is she looking for reassurance, sympathy or what? She is certainly making it more difficult for herself to succeed. Would it not be more prudent to say something interesting about her stamp collection before going out quietly to buy a simple cookbook. The time might come when she arranges a small dinner party, produces an 'impossible' soufflé or a perfect pavlova and surprises herself even more than she surprises her friends.

If our message to ourselves is 'You'll never do it', you may be sure we shall live up to this suggestion. Obediently our subconscious mind will respond, and naturally we shall fail. If we doubt our own ability, we actually prevent achievement. If a task is approached with positive, constructive thought, more may be achieved than we ever dared to hope.

Before meeting demanding situations

Think ahead, prepare as far as possible and then justifiably feel you have done your best.

It still remains true that one needs to be very strong-minded to continue without at least some encouragement from other people. We are not all Florence Nightingales or Hannibals.

Remember the successes, remember the positive improvements (even look back to six months ago and find it difficult to believe how much better you are meeting the challenge of hearing loss) and then tell yourself, quite truthfully, that you are growing every day in confidence and in improving your ability.

Once we have found and have faith in our real selves and have found the inner confidence and inner strength we need, we shall have a reservoir of quiet certainty without making further efforts.

Final thoughts

1. Never be afraid of failure. Everyone makes mistakes. Those who don't fail often are unlikely to make anything.
2. It is a wise man who learns from other men's mistakes, but a wiser man who learns from his own.

3.   If the sun or moon should doubt,
       They'd immediately go out.   (Blake)

4. Concentrate on CCPA. This is something one should practise continuously. What do the initials stand for? Courage, Confidence and a Positive Approach.

5. There is a sense in which outer power is an illusion; inner strength can change the world.

Remember: confidence is catching, confidence is crucial, confidence can be cultivated.

Don't allow unjust criticism to disturb you; it may be a disguised compliment.

Sixteen sentences

Sixteen sentences which, said unhurriedly before going to sleep, will encourage a positive approach (with acknowledgements to Dr Antony Waba):

As from today I am going to feel physically stronger and fitter in every way.

I will feel more alert ... more wide-awake ... more energetic.

I will become much less easily tired ... much less easily fatigued ... much less easily discouraged ... much less easily depressed.

Every day ... I will become so deeply interested in whatever I am doing ... in whatever is going on around me ... my mind will become completely distracted away from myself.

Every day ... my mind will become calmer and clearer ... more composed ... more placid ... more tranquil ... I will become much less easily worried ... much less easily agitated ... much less easily fearful and apprehensive ... much less easily upset.

I will be able to think more clearly ... I will be able to concentrate more easily.

I will be able to give my whole undivided attention to whatever I am doing ... to the complete exclusion of everything else.

Consequently ... my memory will rapidly improve ... and I will be able to see things in their true perspective ... without magnifying my difficulties ... without ever allowing them to get out of proportion.

Every day ... I will become emotionally much calmer ... much more settled ... much less easily disturbed.

Every day ... I will become ... and I will remain ... more and more completely relaxed ... and less tense each day ... both mentally and physically.

And as I become ... and as I remain ... more relaxed ... and less tense each day ... so I will develop much more confidence in myself ... more confidence in my ability to do ... not only what I have to do each day ... more confidence in my ability to do whatever I ought to be able to do ... without fear of failure ... without fear of consequences ... without unnecessary anxiety ... without uneasiness.

Because of this ... every day ... I will feel more and more independent ... more able to stick up for myself ... to stand upon my own feet ... to hold my own ... no matter how difficult or trying things may be.

Every day ... I will feel a greater feeling of personal well being ... a greater feeling of personal safety ... and security ... than I have felt for a long, long time.

And because all these things will begin to happen ... exactly as I have been told they will happen ... more and more rapidly ... powerfully ... and completely ... I will feel much happier ... much more contented ... much more optimistic in every way.

I will consequently become much more able to rely upon ... to depend upon ... myself ... my own judgement ... my own opinions. I will feel much less need ... to have to rely upon ... or to depend upon ... other people.

WHATEVER THE TROUBLE IS, FACE IT, DON'T RUN AWAY.[15]

If you run away
it will get
bigger and BIGGER.

Face it,
and it will
come down
to life size.

Ask what is the worst thing that can happen?
What am I really frightened of?
Many of the worst things

NEVER HAPPEN

I DON'T KNOW what to do or what to say, so I shan't say anything
nor do anything, but just

GET ON WITH THINGS.

At least once every hour during the day, I am going to let my whole
body RELAX, just for a moment; take a deep breath and

STOP GETTING WORKED UP.

14. Tinnitus – Noises in the Head or Ears

Why is this in any way connected with speechreading?

Tinnitus can be a cause of worry, tension and anxiety. Tinnitus can interfere with concentration and add to fatigue. Some people find that by thinking about head noises they become worse; by consciously giving them attention they are less easily forgotten. If you are one of these people, I suggest that you stop reading this and move on to the next chapter.

Who has tinnitus?

Noises in the head or ears are experienced by almost everybody to some extent.

It has been found that ninety-eight per cent of young adults (with normal hearing) in a sound-proof room can 'hear something', mostly the sound of steam or a ringing noise. However, they would not necessarily have been conscious of this if they were in an ordinary environment with normal background sounds.

Many people who have no hearing loss at all, people who have very acute hearing, experience tinnitus and may find it hard to tolerate.

It is estimated that two-thirds of those with impaired hearing suffer from tinnitus, but it is almost unknown in the born deaf who have never experienced sound. A survey over one year at Link showed that only 11·8 per cent of deafened people attending courses did *not* have tinnitus.

Two-thirds of a random sample of 54 of those with tinnitus showed that they found it disturbing, 72 per cent experienced it continuously, 18·5 per cent frequently and only 9·25 per cent occasionally. Forty per cent of those experiencing it occasionally found it disturbing.

What is tinnitus? Where does it come from? What is it like?

A formal definition of subjective tinnitus is given by Mr Stewart Mawson in his book *Diseases of the Ear*.[16] He says: 'Tinnitus (Latin for *ringing*) is the name given to the subjective (heard only by the person concerned) experience of hearing sounds in the ear or head which have no basis of reality in the environment, that is to say, the sound cannot be accounted for by vibrations coming from objects external to the patient.'

Objective tinnitus that other people can hear is very rare. I know of one child who had it and who had to plug the offending ear before going to school, otherwise it gave out an audible whistle which disturbed other children although the child was not aware of it himself.

Where does tinnitus come from? Tinnitus is the result of some unwanted stimulation of the nerve of hearing (the auditory-vestibular nerve). Much research is going on to discover causes and treatment. It is a complex subject.

Tinnitus may be very mild and happen only occasionally, present only if attention is given to it, or it may be violently disrupting and at times almost unbearable.

Tinnitus varies. Some people may 'hear' the Niagara Falls in their right ear and Euston Station in their left; tinnitus may be like a continuous high-pitched whistle or the rhythmic sound of a repeated loud, squelchy thump. It may sound like an intermittent road drill combined with a jet plane.

A hidden handicap

In the past tinnitus received very little attention, and the distress it could cause went almost unrecognized.

Being invisible, there is nothing to show, and although most people have occasional ringing in the ears, or other noises, very loud or continuous tinnitus is likely to be outside their experience. The sufferer meets with incredulity from friends and relations: 'It's in your imagination' or 'Of course there's no banging or whistling going on. I can't hear it.'

The sufferer himself may be worried that he is 'hearing things which aren't there'. It is easy to be alarmed by something which one imagines does not happen to other people and which one's family and friends may suggest is pure imagination or, worse still, the first sign of madness!

The fear of tinnitus, and the difficulty of sharing the fear with even one's nearest and dearest, can be almost as upsetting as tinnitus itself.

Tinnitus is *not* just imagination. To quote a current RNID leaflet on the subject: 'Tinnitus sufferers are perhaps the least understood group and there are some doctors who consider these patients to be simply neurotic. THIS IS NOT THE CASE, the noises are real and are generated by the inner ear.'

Learning to live with it

Naturally, if tinnitus is troublesome, you will seek medical advice, but in only a few cases (it is suggested less than five per cent) is there a simple remedy where the cause of tinnitus is in the outer or middle ear. Sometimes the only advice which can be given is, 'Learn to live with it.' Try to cultivate an attitude of mind which will make it as tolerable as possible. This is largely an individual matter.

Keep a diary and note if any particular pattern emerges, if any circumstances can be connected with increase or decrease of the tinnitus.

Worrying about, concentrating on and listening to the head noises will make them seem even more prominent and dominating. If the sufferer thinks and talks of nothing else, friends and acquaintances will become bored and talk to someone else, which will not help tinnitus or help improve speechreading skills.

Solutions vary. In one small group Mrs M finds that alcohol helps her forget the noises and is in real danger of 'taking to the bottle', whereas Mrs N finds that even a thimbleful of alcohol increases the head noises dramatically. Mr L and the man next to him found the noises did not interfere with sleep but were worse on waking. Miss O was awake most of the night pacing the room and making herself cups of tea. Several people found that relaxation helped. One person could cope provided that she was always doing things. Mr X found the sound of running water reduced his tinnitus; on bad days he spent much time in the bathroom. Another sufferer plunged her face into cold water for relief.

Some people find it helpful to listen to the noises and to try to be selective, to turn them into a tune or a rhythm. Other people can forget them almost entirely if their mind is fully absorbed and concentrating wholly on something else. A totally absorbing hobby may work wonders. Sufferers who turn to alcohol or smoking may actually increase the tinnitus as well as causing additional problems.

Although it may seem utterly unlikely, sometimes one can 'make friends' with tinnitus. As I am writing these words, I have a persistent, low-pitched hum in my left ear. It comes in the evening after a busy day and tells me that it is past my bed-time. 'Ah!' I say to myself. 'There's Charlie again. I suppose I should knock off.' Fortunately, 'Charlie' is a mild noise, like a small aeroplane, not the sound of a jet at close range. 'Charlie' acts like a welcome in-built warning system, an alarm clock in reverse.

Some people find it impossible to sleep a wink on a long night journey in a train. 'It's the noise,' they say. 'I couldn't possibly sleep through it.' Other people may settle down happily: the noise means a safe background, a train on its way – eating the miles, with a rhythm and vibration which could be thought of as a loud, comforting lullaby. Such a traveller may sleep soundly and awaken refreshed – that is, unless the train stops and the sudden silence wakes him.

At the Link Centre a four-day residential study was arranged for deafened people who were finding tinnitus a major handicap. The object was to discover if ways could be found to make it easier to live with. In the general discussion at the end the group agreed that:

1. Among the factors increasing tinnitus were worry, anxiety, apprehension, tension and generally feeling upset.

2. Some people found that being in a crowd aggravated tinnitus. They suggested the reasons were trying to find out who was speaking and looking quickly from one person to another with rising anxiety. Increased apprehension in such a difficult situation increased tension.

3. Everyone agreed that tinnitus was worse when they were tired, particularly when they were mentally tired rather than physically tired.

One or two people had felt afraid of the head noises, and everyone agreed that there was a need to have tinnitus explained and that professional workers, such as occupational therapists, lip-reading teachers, general practitioners and so on should be aware of the effect of tinnitus and the reality of the complaint. This book would not be complete without providing you with some information on the subject.

The Tinnitus Masker is a fairly new innovation which provides relief to many (but not all) sufferers. The masker (works like a behind-the-ear hearing-aid) produces a constant sound which can be increased until it is louder than the head noises. Being a more acceptable sound, it is easier to live with than the tinnitus. Maskers are on sale through hearing-aid dispensers and may be prescribed under the NHS. Of course the masker is only useful when the user has some hearing.

The British Tinnitus Association was formed on 9 July 1979. In July 1982 it was estimated that 300,000 people in the UK suffered from tinnitus which interfered with their ability to lead normal lives. The weight of numbers is revealing; at the very least it witnesses to the reality of tinnitus.

Those who join a local tinnitus group may find that being with others who know the problems and can share their experiences is comforting, even reassuring.

An excellent cassette of simulated tinnitus is available from RNID. People who do not suffer from tinnitus are usually astonished and say, wide-eyed, 'I had no idea it could be like that.'

Some people prefer not to talk or to think about their tinnitus as they find that the more they concentrate on it the worse it becomes.

There are many different causes of tinnitus and one's own tolerance can vary. It is easier to cope with any difficulty when feeling well and alert, less easy when worried, tired, 'out of sorts'. There are many excellent books available on tinnitus.

It is helpful to realize that tinnitus is now widely recognized; courses are run for professional people who meet tinnitus sufferers; there is much research which is continuing.

15. Giddiness and Loss of Balance

Close connection of hearing and balance

The balance mechanism consists of three semi-circular canals, or small loops which are at right angles to each other, a convenient arrangement covering three dimensions.

Any movement of the head changes the position of the semi-circular canals in relationship to gravity and so tells the owner which way up he is and gives him general orientation. There are small scraps of calcium ('otholites' or 'ear-stones') which perch on top of little hairs. Their weight, although so small, responds to the force of gravity, and the little hairs they balance upon are sensitive to their movement. In the ordinary way, it's all part of the service.

What has this to do with hearing? The whole apparatus is part of the inner ear, and the total system works in the same fluid which also surrounds the cochlear (that is the part of the inner ear with 20,000–25,000 minute hairs which respond to sound waves). It is the auditory-vestibular nerve which serves both hearing and balance. So with this close affinity it is not surprising that, when loss of balance is caused by some disturbance of that labyrinth-like mechanism, it also may be associated with hearing loss.

If the fluid pressure in which the system works is upset, this is a very uncomfortable experience, as anyone who has been seasick will confirm; luckily things quickly return to normal when one totters onto dry land, white and shaken.

Giddiness and loss of balance have many different causes. Sometimes they are associated with ringing in the ears and fluctuating hearing. The giddiness may also be accompanied by a feeling of nausea and actual sickness.

To a great extent eyes are able to take over the function of keeping us upright because we are able to orientate ourselves by seeing our own position in relation to the world around.

Living with giddiness

An attack may be totally sudden or there may be prior warning. Giddiness may be brought on by watching a twirling ballet dancer, the flicker of zigzag, rapid movement of an out-of-tune television or the quick flickering of bright lights. Avoid looking at such things as much as possible.

When crossing the road, one needs to look each way quickly and often several times. Make a point of crossing where there is a central bollard. This will mean that you have to look only one way for the oncoming traffic. Reach the bollard which gives you the opportunity to pause, and take your time before you look in the opposite direction and cross the other half of the road. Always aim to look first one way and then the other, move both head and shoulders together in the direction in which you want to look; avoid turning the head. The seven points below are taken from *Living With Giddiness*,[17] a leaflet prepared by Mrs M. Seiffert MCP, for Link, the British Centre for Deafened People.

1. Do not move your head quickly.
2. When picking something up from the floor, stand slightly in front and to the side of the object; then, keeping the head upright, bend the knee and, still looking forward, pick up the object by feel; do not look down.
3. When sitting down, tense your tummy muscles immediately before rising, with one foot further back than the other taking most of your weight; rise without a quick jerky movement and, when upright, stand for a moment and take a deep breath before starting to walk away.
4. When getting out of bed, do not hurry. Swing legs one side of the bed and then sit up. Stay sitting on the bed for a few moments, then follow procedure as for 3 above.
5. When walking, look up; fix eyes on a distant spot; do not watch your feet or the pavement.
6. When standing for any length of time, remember that a wide base is more stable than a small one. Do not stand on one foot; stand with feet apart, weight evenly distributed.
7. Watching rapid movements can aggravate giddiness. For example, in a fast-moving train it is better to look at the horizon than at the close landscape – it is even better to avoid looking out of the window.

Helpful exercises

Do these exercises whilst looking into a long mirror and do them smoothly. Take your time.

Arm exercises

Standing with arms downwards.
1. Without bending elbows, raise arms forward to shoulder height; drop to sides.
2. Repeat as 1 but, when dropping arms, continue movement to extend arm sideways to shoulder height. Swing down and forward rhythmically to shoulder height; and repeat.

Leg exercises

Standing with arms downwards.
1. Mark time by raising knees alternately.
2. Without bending knees, raise legs forward alternately with toes pointed. Pause before returning to ground.
3. Without bending knees, raise legs sideways alternately. Pause before returning to ground.

Body balance

1. With feet apart and hands on hips, bend slowly to left – to upright position – to right.
2. Stand on one leg with hands on hips, and repeat 1.

Sometimes it is possible to decide what particular activities bring on an attack of giddiness. Again, keep a diary and note if any particular pattern emerges. Mrs T finds that a particular type of neon light upsets her balance. This light is used in deep-freeze displays in particular supermarkets; it makes her pitch forward into the deep-freeze container. She now goes to the friendly corner shop instead. The same lady suffers loss of balance when she looks down. Being fond of tapestry work, this was frustrating until her husband made her an adjustable frame so that she could work her tapestry at eye level.

Giddiness and loss of balance can be very disrupting. Attacks may come on suddenly with little warning. It may even give passers-by the impression of drunkenness, which is why some people carry a card or note to say, 'I suffer from bad attacks of giddiness.' Fortunately many people have some warning before an attack.

An SOS talisman is obtainable at many chemists. Worn in the form of a gilt or silvered bracelet or necklace, it provides information about the wearer in cases of accident or illness. It is recognized in thirty-five countries and looks like a piece of jewelley but is useful in cases of emergency. Perhaps you, too, may decide to wear one.

16. Amplified Vibration, Speechreading and Communication

This chapter is about possible ways in which amplified vibration (vibro-tactile aids) may help.

Sound is all a matter of vibration transmitted through the air from some object. When a sound is low-pitched, the vibration can actually be seen and felt. The lowest open string on a 'cello vibrates as the sound is made; put your finger gently on the string and you will feel the tickle of the vibration. This is even more pronounced on a double bass which has even lower-pitched notes. But it will not be obvious on a violin or even on the upper register of a 'cello because the higher pitched the sound, the faster and smaller the vibrations become.

Only the ear (not the skin) is able to detect vibrations that are above eight hundred cycles per second. Therefore amplified vibration on the skin gives only information about low-pitched sounds. It may give awareness of traffic and slamming doors but certainly will not respond to a skylark.

Some materials absorb vibration more than others. Put your hand on a wooden pew in a church when the organ is in full throttle and you will feel some of the low-pitched vibrations of the music. On the other hand, soft furnishings, foam rubber and so on absorb sound and will not transmit any information through vibration even if the organ explodes. Some people who have become severely deafened do not wear rubber soles on their shoes because they can only feel the vibration through the floor when wearing leather soles.

My personal experience of using amplified vibration

When hearing loss in adult life is very severe or total, there is more sensitivity to vibration. Not everyone finds amplified vibration an asset to speechreading: it may be a distraction, an interference with the concentration needed to 'get the message'. Others find that amplified vibration opens a whole new field of perception, an added dimension from which information can be gathered.

In my experience, response to amplified vibration is immediate and definite. Either, 'No. It is an unhelpful distraction' or 'Yes, yes' and it is welcomed with enthusiasm, even with delight.

The possibilities of amplified vibration first dawned on me in 1972 when James Yates, who had become totally deafened, was referred to Link. He had been a keen dancer before losing his hearing, and we talked about feeling vibrations of the music on the dance floor through the soles of one's feet. James discussed this with a technical officer, and together they converted a very powerful hearing-aid (now useless to James) into an amplifier of vibration which could be felt.

It took very little ingenuity to transform an ordinary bone conductor type of National Health hearing-aid and to attach a metal ring to the receiver so that it could be worn like an ordinary ring. The hand closed over the receiver picked up vibration, and the cord to the microphone went up the wearer's sleeve unobtrusively. We christened the device 'Tactile Link' (TL for short).

TL was laughably uncomplicated, but, in spite of not being specially designed, it had the splendid advantage of being readily available. The metal ring attached to the vibrating receiver was cheap because one of the users made rings of different sizes by cutting up little sections of copper piping of different-sized bore. The metal ring was superseded by a strip of VELCRO around the finger, which interfaces with VELCRO attached by superglue to the vibrating receiver.

In spite of its simplicity, the TL proved to be very helpful. Ever since 1972 some people attending Link courses have been successfully introduced to it.

In 1979 a residential working party of users was arranged to talk about their practical experiences with the TL. The findings were summarized and published. It led me to ponder two questions. (1) Why was not amplified vibration generally available to those few people who were likely to benefit? (2) Was James Yates really the very first person in the world to think about and use it?

World developments

In 1980 a summary of research throughout the world was produced as part of a large technical volume, *Sensory Aids for the Hearing Impaired* (Free Press of New York). This showed that as long ago as 1923 a research worker drew attention to the usefulness of vibration to aid speechreading. Interest was stimulated. A single vibrator similar to TL was used in the USA in the 1920s by a worker called Gault.

With it some people were able to identify any one of 120 sentences. In the 1970s a worldwide seminar on the use of vibration was held in Japan.

The worldwide progress in using vibration to aid understanding speech was summarized in 1974 by Kirkman. Much of the recorded research seemed to be on the ability (or non-ability) to distinguish different sounds or single words through the tactile sense, mainly with deaf children in mind. Recently there has been an upsurge of interest in its use with deafened adults.

Strangely, there did not seem to be much on-going practical application in the early days. It was strange, too, that knowledge of this work was not mentioned in the training of people like me who became qualified to teach lip-reading. In the 1970s some further experiments in the USA added electrodes to the skin. This gave an additional but different response to sound (a tingling feeling) in addition to the sensation of vibration (as shown in a paper prepared for a research conference on 'Speech-processing aids for the deaf' by Scott, Defilippo, Sach and Miller, of St Louis).

The Swedish vibrator, wrist-worn, was the first purpose-designed instrument which became generally available in UK followed by the British vibro-tactile instruments which are now available in this country.

Practical application

The 1979 Working Party on vibration organized by the LINK CENTRE convinced me that amplified vibration has great potential for some (but not all) profoundly deafened people. (1) in providing information from the world around; (2) in assisting communication with people. Although it is the second aspect which concerns speechreaders, you may be interested to share some discoveries made by the 1979 study group from their own experience, and from experience at the Link Centre since 1972.

Perhaps one of the most valuable assets of TL is restoring some tangible contact with the environment, although only to a limited extent. People see in an objective way, they see things 'out there' in front of their face. Your eyes look out into the world around you. Not so with hearing and vibration. In contrast hearing and vibration provide information *from* objects and people which 'comes in' to you and impinges on you. The different has significance. Sight provides the dimension of space – hearing (and vibration) the dimension of time.

If hearing loss is sudden, and it is severe or total, the withdrawal of this background information happens instantaneously. This deprivation of information coming in from the environment can be the cause of vague unease, of insecurity and feelings of depression.

On trying the TL for the first time, more than one recently deafened person has said with astonishment, 'The world has come alive again.' This may be an emotional experience, so trial should be on an individual basis and not within a group.

Even limited information from the environment is useful. Different degrees of vibration of passing traffic may indicate if it is a small Fiat or a ten-ton lorry; it will be a more normal situation than watching different-sized vehicles drifting silently by.

Use of Tactile Link with the telephone (as reported at 1979 Link study)

1. Lift the telephone and hold the microphone next to the telephone earpiece. You should be able to feel the dial tone burr.
2. Dial the number. Unless the number is engaged, the ringing pulses will be felt.
3. When the person called lifts the receiver, the ringing pulses will cease. The person called will normally speak first (which of course cannot be heard). After a very slight pause you identify yourself: 'This is ... speaking.'
4. You ask questions which will entail 'Yes' or 'No' answers. The person called responds by giving one sharp tap on or near the receiver's telephone mouthpiece for 'Yes', two taps for 'No'.

The person who receives the call must know the procedure beforehand, the person making the call needs to prepare questions for the Yes/No reply.

Example of a telephone call to a friend

Caller – This is Sheila speaking, is that Molly?
Reply – *Two taps*
Caller – Is Molly at home?
Reply – *One tap*
Caller – Can I have a word with her?
Reply – *One tap*
Caller – Is that Molly?
Reply – *One tap*

Caller – I have been asked to do teas at the tennis club on Saturday. Will you be there?
Reply – *One tap*
Caller – Will you give me a hand?
Reply – *One tap*
Caller – The bunfight starts at 4 p.m. Can you be there at 3.30?
Reply – *Two taps*
Caller – Can you manage four o'clock?
Reply – *One tap*
Caller – Splendid! Is George better?
Reply – *One tap*
Caller – Is he out of hospital yet?
Reply – *Two taps*
Caller – Bad luck – give him our best wishes.
Reply – *One tap*
Caller – By the way, will you bring a teacloth with you on Saturday?
Reply – *One tap*
Caller – Thanks. Luckily someone has offered to do the washing up. Cheerio, see you at four on Saturday.

The speechreader has obtained accurate information through 'yes' and 'no' answers to specific questions.

Amplified vibration from the world around

Some people find they can distinguish between the vibration pattern made by people talking, running water, a knock at the door, footsteps, music. However, vibration of sounds at 800 cycles per second and below is the limit of information, the vibrator picks up unwanted sounds which may drown the signals which you want to receive.

A practical use is to give warning, if someone enters the room a few hand claps or knock at the door may alert you to their presence; the shock of someone approaching you silently is avoided. It can be useful in traffic if one can distinguish between a mini-car and a ten-ton lorry approaching; on a train journey, the vibration can reveal when breaks are applied and the train is slowing down.

There are several devices for home use which rely on vibration, for example, the pocket-sized timer, so useful if the warning 'ping' of the oven timer cannot be heard. The special smoke detector which produces vibration as well as flashing light, is surely a 'must' if anyone lives alone.

Wearing a vibrator receiver has unexpected possibilities. A ring receiver worn by a deaf football player responded to a remote control signal from the referee.

Used with a metal detector a vibrator has given excellent results to more than one enthusiast. An article published by *Treasure Hunting Manual* was written by one user with profound hearing loss, who claimed that it was 100% successful.

Amplified vibration as an aid to communication

There is no doubt that amplified vibration can provide dramatic assistance in acquiring speed speechreading for some people with profound hearing loss.

How? The speed speechreader is aiming to follow normal speech (not specially adapted speech). He has natural speech/language experience to link all the signals he receives in his aural memory. The natural rhythm of speech is already familiar. Though he is already aware of speech through sound (or memory of sound)/appearance/ sensation, amplified vibration provides reinforcement from yet one more source.

Amplified vibrations used in SAS practice

Once more the secret is to learn-by-doing, to make the TL part of that do-it-yourself mirror practice which is daily routine. Amplified vibration can reinforce the normal rhythm of speech and can greatly assist forming the right habits. It picks up all low-pitched noise, and so it should be used in quiet circumstances, on your own. Later it may possibly be used in ordinary conversation, but again quiet circumstances avoid interference from the background noise.

In your do-it-yourself practice you have already been talking aloud to yourself. Feel vibration from your own voice through the vibrator; don't think about it or analyse how it happens – just let it happen. Start by concentrating on your familiar day-to-day sentences. Then become more venturesome. Rhythm of speech can be felt through amplified vibration.

Here is the rhythm of a nursery rhyme, tap this out, or clap it:

```
 − . − . − . −
. − . − . − .
 − . − . − . −
. − . − . − .
```

Is it the first verse of 'Three Blind Mice' or 'Mary, Mary Quite Contrary' or 'Jack and Jill'? Could you spot which from the rhythm?

Having discovered which it is, say it up-to-time at normal speed. Tap out the rhythm of other verses you know. Some people have had great pleasure and good practice from the rhythm of songs which were familiar before losing their hearing – such old friends as 'Auld Lang Syne', 'God Save the Queen' and the Wedding March.

Think for a moment of the difference in rhythmic pattern of these three songs. Which has the rhythm of:

A   – – . –
                      – – . –

Which one has the rhythm of:

B   – – – – . .
                      – – – – . .
                      – – – –

Yes, A was 'Here Comes the Bride' (clap it out for yourself to prove it) and B was 'God Save the Queen'. Now you can tap out the rhythm of 'Auld Lang Syne'; sing it at the same time if you like. After all, you have locked the door before starting your practice, and you have explained to people that your programme is not silent.

Part of your practice material with the TL should be selected not only for the rhythm but also the emotional feeling – the stress and pauses – of the whole utterance.

There is much great prose and poetry to be enjoyed in this way and to provide endless and valuable practice material, but *it must be memorized first*. You cannot concentrate on reading from a book and also on SAS 'listening' with undivided attention.

The use of non-colloquial speech in this way as practice material is to develop a particular skill. Of course people don't talk like this, but by concentrating on whole sentences the amplified vibration reinforces and strengthens the rhythm and sensation of speech.

Choose the practice passage for the way the thought is expressed; say it aloud, thinking of the rhythm, feeling and emotional impact. Here is an example spoken by David when he is told that his son has been killed:

> But the king covered his face
> and the king cried with a loud voice
> O my son Absalom,
> O Absalom, my son, my son.

Think again of these words. What anguish they express! Where is the natural pause as you say this sentence? The Authorized Version of the Bible provides a fund of marvellous examples, a quality which is lost in many modern translations.

The prose used in *Lord of the Rings* and other Tolkien books has the same feeling for words. Sometimes the words themselves mean little, but the emotional impact they convey goes deeper than the intellect. Winston Churchill's writings and speeches have the same quality of speaking not only to the mind but to the heart. (See Chapter 9, 'Living Language'.)

Why do I recommend this type of DIY practice? Through experience. One example is a deafened Link guest who in 1974 went home with a TL and practised with it on his own for $1\frac{1}{4}$ hours every evening after supper as a regular routine. Being a Freemason, he had to memorize a great deal of material, and he did this with TL in his do-it-yourself SAS study. He became an amazingly proficient speed speechreader.

Miss D was also an excellent speed speechreader. She lost her hearing totally and suddenly. She particularly liked the long poem 'The Ancient Mariner' and memorized it. She said bits of it to herself aloud every day. This combination of using aural memory with appearance and feeling of speech was a source of enjoyment. You probably know some of the lines already: '... and ice mast high, came floating by, as green as emerald'. Great rhythm for TL practice.

Use the rhythm and stress which come naturally when you speak what you have memorized; if you think of the meaning being conveyed, there will be natural pauses and natural emphasis to be absorbed subconsciously.

Having reached that stage, it may be useful to compare some rhythmic patterns in more detail. Have you noticed the particular pattern, for example, for different months of the year?

Say the same sentence, ending with a different month, like this:

A. My birthday is on the first of –

What could that last month be? Only three months fit that particular rhythmic pattern – March, May, June.

B. Try the sentence again, finished with the rhythm: – .

Two months are possible – which?

C. Repeat, changing the rhythm to: . – .

Now four months have the same pattern. Can you spot them?

D. Once more. This time the rhythm of the last word is – . . .

Only two months will fit this pattern.

E. Say the sentence for the last time.

The following pattern applies to only one month and the rhythm is: . –

Answers

A. March, May, June (you knew this anyway).
B. April, August.
C. September, October, November, December.
D. January, February.
E. July.

Now say a sentence which finishes by naming a member of the Royal Family: 'Have you ever been introduced to – – . ?' Notice the rhythm of the different name you insert each time. Clap it if you like. Which names have the same rhythm? Prince Philip – – . (above) is different from . – . – (the Prince of Wales). Which other differences and similarities can you spot?

You can extend this kind of exercise almost endlessly, but it is vitally important to use the form of the same complete up-to-time sentence for each exercise, leaving only the last bit that changes.

Remember – *always* the entire sentence and *always* up to time.

Amplified vibration and voice volume

When one cannot hear the loudness of one's own voice, there is difficulty in modulating voice volume according to background noise. A small noise-level indicator can give some guidance about the volume of background noise (which of course you cannot hear).

Vibrators should not be issued indiscriminately but with appropriate supervision and training.

The sensation of amplified vibration used in conjunction with a sound-level meter and a chart to show the relative loudness of different sounds (from a whisper to a jet aeroplane) is a useful combination.

If the room is quiet (as shown by the sound-level meter), then a voice which produced 80 decibels – that is, about the level of heavy street traffic – would obviously be far too loud. With lowered voice the vibrator could be felt to be less active, and the sound-level meter would show the lower volume of sound. The physical effort required in speaking would also be less than against a background noise of heavy traffic. Even when the sound-level meter is not available, the physical effort of talking and the strength of the signals from the vibrator may still give useful clues, although the loudness of background noise would not be shown visibly.

Experimentally the vibrator design has been improved and incorporates the three-speed switch for quiet, medium and loud, controlled by the user.

Summary

Amplified vibration has many possibilities. Six points to bear in mind are:

1. It picks up all low-pitched sounds but not high-pitched sounds.
2. It responds not only to wanted sounds but also to unwanted background noise.
3. It may restore, to some extent, tangible contact with the world around.
4. As an aid to speechreading it does not help everyone who becomes deafened as an adult. For some people it may be an unwanted distraction; for others it may be an exciting and invaluable asset.
5. It may be used to help control voice volume.
6. It can greatly assist some deafened people to become speed speechreaders.

17. For Friends, Family and Other People who meet Speechreaders

I wonder why you are reading this chapter? Perhaps someone in your family, a friend or a neighbour does not hear well. Perhaps you repeat what you say or raise your voice. In spite of your efforts, there may be mishearing and misunderstandings.

Hearing loss can be difficult for speaker and listener. Sometimes you may feel that it is really not worth repeating what seems trivial or unimportant; the effort is tiring, even exhausting.

Those whose nearest and dearest suffer hearing loss are offered very little assistance to meet the situation! Take heart! Read on! A few very simple suggestions can make life easier for you both.

Acquiring insight

We hear from before birth and go on hearing continuously all the time. Sound comes from all directions, round corners, through darkness, even during sleep. It takes imagination to understand what is needed when sounds become muffled, distorted, unclear or even non-existent.

Notice how many people you speak with before bedtime; how easy it is to relax and half listen; how often conversation is tossed about with questions, laughter, interjections, interruptions and general verbal ping-pong. Imagine the concentration needed if you could fully understand only one person at a time, the person you could see. Imagine how difficult it is to look at the speaker if you cannot tell the direction the voice is coming from, or if you cannot hear his voice and maybe don't know he is speaking.

Switch off the TV sound and watch the newsreader; do this every night for a week. At first he may look funny chatting away silently but it soon becomes a bore.

Notice sounds from the world around. They give information or warning. Simple things like the rain on the window pane, the cat mewing to come in or the noise of a bus which could be on top of you before it is seen. Notice the vital few words with the people at the garage, the bank, the booking-office, the doctor's surgery. Imagine what it is like to sit through a meeting, go to the theatre or try to follow a further education class if it is essential to see the speaker's face in order to understand what is said.

Communication is a partnership

Communication is an activity in which there is a sharing of thoughts, ideas, information, feelings, so that they are understood. Two people are involved. One of them is you.

However good one's hearing may be the amount that is understood greatly depends upon you.

Communication is a sharing, when you are speaking you can be an 'aid to hearing' which costs absolutely nothing but which can be a priceless asset.

People who don't hear well 'listen with their eyes'. Be sure that they are looking at your face before you start talking. Gain attention first, make sure there is a clear view of your face.

The validity of what is said is often judged by the expression of the eyes. Face-to-face conversation is easiest to understand. Whether or not one hears well the face of the speaker helps to convey their message.

This means one must avoid calling from another room, talking with your face in shadow, walking away before you have finished the sentence or calling something over your shoulder as you go out of the door.

Strategy to help you both

If visiting someone with hearing loss write first giving date, time and reason for visit, arrive punctually. This saves explanations, searching for hearing aid and general inconvenience.

Aim for quiet circumstances without background TV. Close windows if traffic is noisy. Be aware of the possible need for privacy, for example, in a hospital ward an intimate conversation with close relatives should not be overheard. It is always wise to write down important points so that there is no risk of misunderstanding.

Gain attention before speaking, then make the subject known at the beginning of the conversation, not at the end when it is too late to

Sorry – no one can speechread
you unless you remove your hand
or the plant.

Please, nurse, explain
before you put on
your mask.

Think before you light that cigarette.

Why not change the hair-do?

Sit facing the window. Then the light will be
on your face, not in the speechreader's eyes.

Do not bob about.
Keep your head still.

It helps when faces are
at the same level

not
  at
    an
      angle.

contribute or to follow the train of thought. Indicate change of subject. NEVER SHOUT. It not only distorts the face but gives the impression of anger or impatience. Speak naturally but at reasonable speed (do not gabble or mumble!) and not too fast! If you are not understood then re-phrase the sentence. For example, 'the weather forecast isn't good, it's going to rain' could be repeated as 'I've brought my umbrella with me because we may have showers.'

Unobtrusive help is needed, make communication easier in tactful ways for example notice the situation when a group is chatting and the risk that one person can be left out – always the one who does not hear well.

MOST IMPORTANT OF ALL be sure that other people speak direct to the person with hearing loss and NOT to you. 'Does he take sugar in his tea?' 'Why not ask him!' It takes a little longer but is time well spent, DON'T JUMP IN YOURSELF WITH THE REPLY.

Going further

One word alone won't make sense. I said to a speechreader, 'What do you think of psychoanalysis?' She looked puzzled and replied, 'I prefer white myself.' It was only then that I realized that 'psychoanalysis' looks very much like 'yellow elastic' on the lips. I should have phrased my question differently: 'In cases of mental illness, what do you think of psychoanalysis as a form of treatment?'

Start with the subject talked about, be logical, come to the point, avoiding unnecessary waffle. Be a clear speaker. Clear speech with crisp consonants is invaluable.

General announcements, group discussions or committees are difficult, the speechreader must look at the right place at the right time. A little unobtrusive assistance by some pre-arranged signal can indicate who is speaking.

Allow time. It may take a little longer to speechread what you say. If you are in a hurry or feel resentful, that will be obvious. Be patient. It is much more effort for the speechreader than it is for you.

Be alert for fatigue – beware of talking 'non-stop', allow a few pauses; when the speechreader is talking it is less tiring for him.

Choose your time. At the end of a day's work, when this has involved meeting people, the speechreader will want to relax and unwind before starting any more conversation.

When someone says, 'Does he drive?', 'Will he have sweet or dry sherry?' or 'Where is the pain he complains of?' make it your golden rule to reply, 'Why not ask him?'

If the person talking is impossible to speechread, he can use pencil and paper. As a last resort, you can repeat the question to the speechreader who will then reply direct. It may be quicker for someone who hears well to reply, particularly when they know the answer and the question is unimportant, but this must be avoided at all cost.

When there is a face-to-face conversation and a third person joins in, the speechreader, who cannot see two people at the same time, tends to become isolated while they chat together. Truly 'two's company, three's none!' You have been in the background, careful *not* to interrupt the *tête-à-tête*, but now, with one more person, the situation changes.

You tactfully join in the conversation with *one* of the three (preferably the newcomer) and therefore restore the one-to-one situation. Be alert to the possibility of change to cross-talk between four people, which is much more difficult for the speechreader.

If, unavoidably, three people are involved in conversation, it will help if the seating arrangements are as follows:

Speechreader X is positioned as advantageously as possible, when two people are talking:

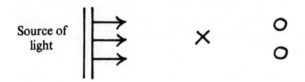

Wrong positioning (below). The speechreader cannot see both speakers unless he keeps turning his head:

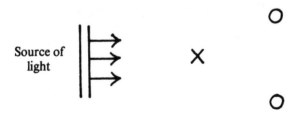

Once a conversation has been interrupted, the train of thought has been broken. Contact has been destroyed if someone thoughtlessly buts in. Get your priorities right; leave handing round the scones or letting in the dogs until later on. Don't pass between the speechreader and the person he is talking with; go round them unobtrusively so that you do not break eye contact. Avoid giving your own opinion or contribution as this would create a three-way conversation highly unsatisfactory for speechreading.

Put rather bluntly, your contribution is to shut up, be patient and prevent distractions. Never mind if it does mean that lunch is ten minutes late.

Speech which is seen but not heard

The speechreader may grasp the meaning quickly but it may be received as bare fact, unadorned and unsoftened by excuses, explanations or reasons.

Someone who hears well might be told: 'Disappointing news I'm afraid. Mary is very sorry that she has to put off coming to dinner tonight. They are not sure about getting a baby-sitter. She wondered if you would mind very much if they came another time. I know it's short notice. She does hope it wouldn't put you out, but she didn't know until yesterday, and you know how unreliable these baby-sitters can be!' The speechreader gets the bare facts – 'Mary isn't coming.'

The possible reasons/explanations/excuses should always be fully explained. (Incidentally, if Mary had thought, she would have slipped in a personal note instead of conveying the message secondhand through someone else.)

Tone of voice, inflection and emphasis can completely change the meaning of what is said.

Speech seen but not heard may be taken literally. Something said in jest, quizzically, sarcastically, as a roundabout way of asking a question, may be taken as a literal statement of fact. Metaphor, simile and figures of speech mislead the speechreader. Because you are alert to that possibility, you will already be expressing your thoughts in a direct way.

Wit

Wit often depends on the use of a single word perhaps used in an unusual way.

I was in a group where the conversation was about winter bedroom slippers, their quality, warmth, price and cost of footwear in general. A speechreader was naturally anticipating something about the price of leather, the usefulness of gumboots – possibly how one hops round the room on one leg pulling them off and so on.

An Irishman said, for no apparent reason, 'I wear a green pullover because in Ireland we have green sheep.' This statement 'out of the blue' naturally was not understood by the speechreader, who wondered why people laughed. The obvious thing was to jot down quickly what had been said so that the speechreader would be 'on beam' and laugh too.

Why was this statement so difficult? It bore no relationship to the subject of the conversation. The key words (in italics) are very difficult to see without helpful context: 'I wear a *green pullover* because in *Ireland* we have *green sheep*.' Lastly, the sentence, which was said with an Irish accent and a 'dead-pan' face, isn't particularly logical.

Natural gestures

Natural gestures are normal and spontaneous. Don't try to change them. However, don't allow them to prevent a good view of the face – for example, the constantly wagging first finger in front of the mouth.

Unnatural gesture used instead of speech is to be avoided. For example, a speechreader was having a perfectly ordinary chat about an art exhibition. The speaker stated that a picture was worth over £100. He then broke the whole continuity of the conversation by waving his ten fingers ten times in front of her! Why? She had no difficulty at all in speechreading that the picture was worth over £100, provided that the sentence as a whole was said naturally with normal speech. The sudden unnatural gestures destroyed the normal speech rhythm.

Background information

Background information comes from many indirect sources – general chatter, radio, TV and so on. For the speechreader, magazines, newspapers, libraries, timetables, maps and books in general are not a luxury but a necessity.

Othere people's reaction to background sounds needs explanation. If the family is sitting round peacefully sipping coffee, someone may suddenly rush out of the room. Is it the telephone? Baby crying? The front door bell? Be sure to explain.

The fact that there is no sound or that no one is talking sometimes needs indicating. Without this information, the speechreader may appear to interrupt rudely or think that something is going on that he is missing.

Misunderstanding

Misunderstandings happen through mishearing. While there is nothing funny about this situation, sometimes the result may be funny. Explain at once to the speechreader what the mistake was so that he can share the joke, otherwise he may feel uncomfortable and puzzled by the reactions to his remark.

Think about the things that may be difficult. Work out if there are any particular situations in which you think you could be helpful, and discuss them with the speechreader.

Be logical, stick to the point, avoid waffle

Why talk? Speech is not an end in itself but is meant to convey something. Speech is a tool of communication.

What are you trying to convey? If you don't know, no one else will.

Come to the point. It is hard work to sort out facts from a lot of woolly detail, worse still if the main word is forgotten in mid-stream.

To illustrate, let us eavesdrop on Mrs Smith: 'I went to that little shop on the corner, you know the one, bought by Miss Thingambob when poor old Mr Whatshisname went to Australia or somewhere with his asthma. Well, they have run out of that bread with the knobbly bits on.' Why not think first of the name of the shop and of the name of the bread, and then say: 'I went to Brown's corner shop, and the wholemeal bread had sold out.'

Exercise. Listen to talks – read articles – then jot down a few headings on what message is being conveyed. Could you have done it more concisely? Clear thinking aids clear speaking.

Be a clear speaker

Have you ever listened to yourself on a tape-recorder? Take the first opportunity of hearing your voice 'from the outside'. It is not the voice volume alone that makes speech understandable. It is also good articulation and crisp, clear consonants.

Exercise. Read aloud. Relish the sound of the words. Read with understanding. Read a paragraph at a time with emphasis to make the meaning clear.

Breath is the vehicle of voice. For breath control:
(a) Breathe in through the nose and out through the mouth, slowly, rhythmically. If your hands are allowed to rest lightly on your lower ribs, you should feel expansion sideways when you breathe in and contraction as you breathe out. Do you?
(b) Take in breath quickly through the mouth and then let it escape in an even hiss. Relax – repeat.

An exercise for use of lips and breath. Breathe in. Breathe out slowly whispering, '1, 2, 3'. Don't use the voice; the words are formed by lips alone. Relax. Do the exercise several times. Repeat, whispering up to eight in an even stream as you breathe out.
Your voice should not be 'swallowed'. Let your breath flow in a relaxed stream when you speak.

Exercise to keep voice forward:
(a) Hum. Can you feel your lips vibrating? Check by slightly parting and closing lips, and feel the vibration as you say mumm mumm mumm.
(b) Say the sound of AH (as in 'far'). You will notice that your jaw will move downwards. Now say AH again and pinch your nose. There should be no difference in the sound when your nose is pinched or not.
Now try another experiment, this time to aid clear articulation. Place some tiny pieces of paper on the back of your hand. With the back of your hand close to your lips, say, 'Pay the piper.' Each time you say the sound 'p', you should make such a little explosion of breath that the bits of paper fly off. Now try again with the sound of 't'. The word 'titter' should scatter your paper twice. Hold your hand near your lips as you say, 'Cut the cake'; feel the draught on your hand every time 'k' is sounded (e.g. 'Be kind to cats', 'The call of the cuckoo').

The whole sentence is the unit of understanding

Talk in sentences, never one word at a time. Speak normally, without exaggeration.

The following situation happened only last week. Mr A (who does not hear well) 'I haven't seen Mr Smith lately, is he alright?' Mr B (who knows Mr A has hearing problems) replied but did not use his voice at all. With exaggerated 'mouthing' said one word 'Edinburgh'.

This was not understood. The speaker, with best of intentions went on repeating 'Edinburgh' more and more loudly and making his face more and more distorted. If, instead, he had replied by a whole sentence – say – 'Mr Smith's away this week, gone up North to see his old mother' this would have been understood whereas a proper name (Edinburgh) out of the blue and with no helpful context isn't easy! In addition it was not surprising that Mr A was totally flummoxed when suddenly there is no voice and somebody begins to make faces instead.

Clear speech whether or not you hear well

Don't be afraid to open your mouth, the sound won't come out otherwise.

It helps if you know which sounds are easy to see and which are more difficult (shown on charts Pages 61 and 72).

Exercise. Hold the back of your hand half-an-inch or so under your jaw and say 'far, far away'. Did your jaw touch your hand? How many times?

Monotony of voice makes listening more difficult and sleep more attractive. Monotony is often caused because the voice is 'all on one note' and has no change of tone.

Exercise. Say 12345, first making your voice go up the scale (you are not singing, just using your speaking voice), then going down the scale. Still saying 12345, make it sound like a question – an invitation – a refusal; say it to express anger – sorrow – joy – simply by changing tone and inflection of the voice.

Circumstances must alter your way of speaking. Be adaptable, be flexible. It is no good speaking to a group in a large room with the same amount of voice that you would use for an intimate cosy chat to a friend close by your side.

Two important factors are loudness and speed. Speak in ordinary conversational voice in a large room or hall and *only the front row will hear you.* Many halls reverberate (echo). If you are going to speak in them, slow down to allow time for the sound to travel. The voice must be projected. How many people who ask questions or speak at small or large gatherings are really only talking to themselves?

Exercise. Read a piece as you would tell a bed-time story to a sleepy six-year-old. Read it again to be heard by eight or ten adults in your sitting-room, and again to be heard in a big hall, allowing time for your voice to travel to the back of the hall.

Distractions get in the way of receiving speech.

Hands that flutter, flap or fiddle; the nervous twitch; repeated sniffing or dangling earrings; the constant movement of the head, the wagging finger etc may fascinate the listener – busy with these details, he won't try to understand what is being said. Be relaxed – be calm – be natural.

Outside distraction, noise or interruptions prevent communication. I remember an interesting speaker at a small meeting whose careful argument no one absorbed because a baby mouse appeared at his feet and washed its whiskers half way through his lecture.

Exercise. Notice things that distract; you can then avoid them or speak again when they stop.

The listener (bless him)

Listening attentively is hard work – even harder work when one cannot hear well.

No one can be forced to listen. They are more likely to make the effort if the subject is interesting and they are alert than when they are tired, hungry or bored.

Understanding takes place in the mind of the receiver. Different people vary in the speed at which they take in what is said. Please pause sometimes. However well and clearly you speak, you will not be understood if you use unfamiliar words. Avoid technical terms or phrases which, although familiar to you, may be unknown to your listener.

The listener is human, so allow him to get a word in edgeways; he too may have a point of view. Communication should be a two-way affair.

Clarity of speech is a boon and a blessing to everyone, particularly to people who cannot hear too well.

Don't talk to the air. Let *your* point of view, *your* wisdom, *your* contribution be understood.

Be a clear speaker.
Be understood.
Be relaxed.
Be calm.
Be natural.

Finally, it helps if you like the person you are talking to. A pleasant genuine smile is a good start.

As Dorothy Parry has pointed out, in the *Journal of Occupational Therapy*, 1971: '... the one disastrous method is to take suggestions such as these and to apply them solemnly and over-earnestly (am I doing this right? Have I remembered to do that?) sometimes kindly people try so hard to get their message across that one would think that they were talking to a mentally backward five-year-old! It is inexcusable to talk to a mature adult as if he or she were a rather dull child.'

Use your initiative, imagination and commonsense. You are not aiming for some exact scientific precision (if absolute precision is needed, you can use pen and paper), but you are meeting and communicating with another adult human being.

Think of the person, not of the deafness, and then enjoy his or her company.

18. Speechreading and the Quality of Life

The way forward will be different for different people, but not all solutions to hearing loss lie solely in the realm of acquired skills and applied technology.

Hearing loss may mean new priorities and new goals. Speechreading should be more than a communication aid; it should enrich your quality of life, perhaps assisting you to become a more observant person, more aware, more alive, with the flexibility to adapt and adjust to new circumstances and with the courage and confidence to persist. You may be surprised to find hidden talents, new opportunities and unexpected ways forward.

Speechreading increases powers of concentration and sharpens the mind wonderfully. An alert mind and trained eye give astute evaluations. High-sounding jargon or pointless platitudes cut little ice when one is alert to the actual message being conveyed. Speechreading develops a sensitive awareness of the speaker, not merely of the words he utters.

New habits

Look critically at your daily routine. Find out your own comfortable rhythm of living and stick to it.

For some people the morning is a time of energetically tackling things which have to be done. Others never seem to be fully awake until midday but begin to sparkle in the evening, their ideal time for decisive action and clear thinking.

Although speechreaders learn the necessity for keen attention and mental focus, it is not humanly possible to focus attention all day. The importance of 'pause' periods, both short and long term, cannot be overstated!

Keep some space around your life when you can be alone, some time when you are not with people. If there is no time to relish and enjoy the uncluttered hour, are you perhaps too busy? Constant activity can easily become an ineffectual nervous twitch.

Some people give the impression that they are driving themselves (and sometimes those around them) in a kind of non-stop desperation! No time to play with the children, no time to take the dog for a walk or to try their hand at painting, boating or simply thoughtfully chewing a straw. No time to live?

Weave some solitude into your routine. Think of solitude as a constructive element. Less time to chatter could mean more time to form considered opinions, to read widely, to think deeply, to recharge your batteries.

Hobbies, holidays and varied interests are not an optional extra but are for refreshment and re-creation, a means to return to the normal routine with renewed vigour and enthusiasm. So do give yourself a break. How easy it is to allow life to be swallowed up by the daily round and so to miss that pause to reflect and to take one's bearings.

See and behold

You may find new perception of the world around. Here is a true story of one chance remark.

As a child I overheard two women talking. One was expecting a baby. The other took a gloomy view of the situation. Why should the poor child be pushed into the world, having been given no choice, no option, no chance of refusal? It was a dismal prospect, what with the strikes and inflation, the endless chores, the daily boredom and the uphill struggle to make ends meet; the whole effort was of doubtful benefit and hardly worth the candle.

It so happened that the mainspring of my clockwork mouse had broken that very morning. I nodded to myself in heartfelt agreement (in those days children did not comment unless asked, and their presence was usually forgotten).

The other woman's reply was totally unexpected. 'On my way here I saw wild roses in the hedge. If my child sees only one wild rose, life will be worth living.'

Such was my astonishment that I stopped kicking the offending mouse and at the first opportunity went to look at the hedgerow. For the first time I saw not a vague pink blob but an exquisite, fragile, jewel-like object. Yes! Perhaps life *was* worth living after all.

But let us return from the philosophic to the nitty gritty.

Reading

Having grown up surrounded (almost bombarded) by spoken language, we rarely think about it. But if in adult life we suffer some hearing loss, then experience of language is the springboard which turns sound into sense. Let us not take it for granted.

Even when hearing loss is not severe, reading keeps one informed, increases vocabulary and adds to the aural memory-bank. The love of words is an extra bonus. Their rhythm, pattern and cadence may be relished in the mind's ear, almost like a form of music.

Mr A and Miss B both lost their hearing as adults. They were very different people. Mr A had a lively curiosity and enquiring mind. He fully used the public library and discovered poetry almost by accident. He memorized pages of it just because he loved it and often recited his favourite bits to himself on those inevitable odd moments of waiting about in queues and so on.

It is more than a coincidence that he is an excellent speed speechreader, a stimulating, well-informed person, recognized by his colleagues as a man of integrity whose opinions are respected.

Miss B was never particularly interested in the world or the people around her. True, she flipped through magazines, particularly the ones with a lot of coloured pictures. She noticed the newspaper headlines and was vaguely aware of advertisements. Her curiosity had never been great, and without nourishment or stimulation it had shrivelled. To her, language seemed to be nothing more than a means of discovering the price of butter or exchanging views about the weather. Lip-reading skills were of little use because her vocabulary had almost died of starvation. Limited interests led to fewer social contacts (one cannot go on and on talking about nothing), and there was no doubt that her aural memory-bank was well in the red.

I was a student when I met Miss B, but I have never forgotten her. The experience made me realize that there is more to speechreading/lip-reading than meets the eye.

Reading is not an optional extra. It is a positive asset to be used. You too can share the thoughts of great minds, the discoveries, inventions and experiences of the thinkers and doers of past and present, the wisdom and history of many generations and different nationalities.

Reading needs to be recognized as just one more part of your overall plan and pattern of tackling hearing loss.

Speechreading

In spite of the limitations of speechreading, it can be a bridge which, used with listening tactics, is the deciding factor in participation in the ordinary community.

The number of people in this country whose hearing has become impaired in adult life is very large indeed. If society is deprived of the skills and abilities of these citizens, then society will be the poorer. All possible aids – technical and tactical – are worth exploring; simple information and preparation should be used to ensure positive and effective participation.

Speechreading/lip-reading groups meet in many towns; the instructors, methods, aims and meeting-places vary. The group may be very large (only recently I heard of one group of over thirty people), but ideally it should be small. It may be on a one-to-one basis or with a couple where one partner has impaired hearing. When provision is made under further education, it is available only as a group activity, often with a minimum number of participants, always for a set period of time, which may be as long as two hours.

The effectiveness of any group should not be narrowly evaluated. A well-run group will include laughter (a therapy in itself), introduce stimulating ideas and provide information, social contact and mutual encouragement.

The environment varies widely, including multi-purpose halls, hospitals, classrooms and social clubs. In my experience the best setting for groups or individuals is a comfortably furnished room, not too reverberant, with plain, unobtrusive decor and a choice of armchairs and upright chairs which are easily shifted depending on the particular grouping needed for the activity (one-to-one discussion, four grouped round a table, two rows facing each other, a circle and so on).

Whatever the surroundings or the group activity, the inevitable tea-break provides a period for spontaneous conversation.

Social clubs especially for hard-of-hearing people may create lasting friendships and opportunities for service. They may do much to restore self-confidence. They may also encourage better provision and help individuals towards full participation in the general community.

New interests

Once you decide to specialize and become something of an expert in any field, you can study through public libraries, further education classes (providing that there is adequate provision for speechreaders), correspondence courses, exhibitions and so on. The Open University runs courses with special provision for people who have impaired hearing. What begins as a solitary pursuit can develop to the stage where you are the local expert.

Once you have reached a knowledgeable level, and modestly let the fact be known, other people will seek you out. It is profoundly true that 'If you follow in secret your own small light, one by one the answering torches gleam.'

Perhaps you can offer to give talks, show slides, put on an exhibition, start a local interest group. You thus come into the activity as the central person – not on the edge of the outside fringe of a circle but as the instigator, the person with expertise to offer. No longer 'poor Joe struggling to speechread' but instead, 'ask Joe. He's the local expert on prehistoric remains in Lower Trumpington – he's started a dig – he might include you if you're lucky. By the way, he likes you to face him when you talk.' It takes time, effort and application, persistence and determination. But it can and does happen.

Naturally you will study the phrases and vocabulary which apply to your new interest, whatever it is, by careful SAS practice first.

> *Good hobbies.* Books, picture galleries, museums, gardening, old time and folk dancing, art, dress, letters, collecting almost anything can be thrilling. Architecture, astronomy, archery, antiques, a never-ending list.
>
> *Look happy* – other people are waiting to be friendly. Holidays are wonderful, lots to see and do. Old buildings to visit, villages to explore, boating, hiking, enjoy every minute.

What would your list include?

Life is for living, do your 'own thing' sometimes. Do not just exist – LIVE for every hour of the day and your life can become fuller than those of very many people who hear well. Are there places you would like to visit? Not necessarily the moon or Mexico but somewhere special nearer home. Perhaps there is some activity you have often thought you would try 'sometime': Is now the opportunity to begin dog-training, jogging, meditation, writing to *The Times* or writing for the radio?

You have already become very observant. Take time to look at and enjoy simple everyday things, time to admire people and places. When did you last see the sunrise? Different every morning and absolutely free!

People who 'listen with their eyes' may also listen with understanding and empathy. I don't believe we 'make' friends, we discover them when we 'listen with our hearts'. If you have found true friends, you have real treasure.

What would your list include?

Everyone has something to contribute to life. It may not be obvious or spectacular, or even recognized by other people, but it may be very significant. The influence of one individual changes the total sum of things. There is no one else in the world with your personality,

May this book be a link between people, part of a chain which does not have a beginning or an end but only forms its beautiful pattern as each piece relates to the others.

Links of pure gold may be forged in the flame of adversity. For people with a profound hearing loss there are bound to be times when speechreading seems to be very hard going, but even in the dark you are still on the way if your aim is clear and your courage bright.

The very experience of survival may create new strengths and deeper perception. Perhaps it may bring with it, too, release from the pressures to be competitive in the scramble for status and material goods and give instead greater ability to value those things which are true and lasting.

May your own volume of experience grow and develop. May there be many unexpected treasures awaiting discovery. And may this book be at least a small stepping-stone on your way.

Without the way there is no going.
Without the truth there is no knowing.
Without the life there is no living.

Best wishes for the journey forward.

References

1 Haggard, Gatehouse and Davis, 'The prevalence of hearing disorders and its implications for services in the United Kingdom', British Journal of Audiology, 15 (1981), pp 241-52

2 *Missing the Message*, Dr R.H. Thouless, (South East Regional Association for the Deaf, 2nd edition 1984)

3 *Speechreading — Lipreading*, Jeffers and Barley (Charles C. Thomas, Illinois, 1972)

4 *The Listening Eye*, D. Clegg (Methuen, London, 1953).

5 *Teach Yourself Lipreading*, O. Wyatt (Teach Yourself Series, O.U.P., 1961)

6 *A Word in Your Eye*, R.F. McCall (South East Regional Association for the Deaf, 8th edition 1983)

7 Scandinavian Audiology, Vol. 1 No. 14 (November 1972), p 157

8 *By Word of Mouth*, P. Pengelley (The Advisory Council for Children with Impaired Hearing, Australia, 1968)

9 *The Baker's Dozen*, Regan and Kellett (Literary Trust, Australian Association for Better Hearing)

10 Illustration of the speech apparatus (after Kenyon and Knott) is reproduced with acknowledgement to *Sensory Aids for the Hearing Impaired*, ed. by Harry Levitt and James M. Pidcett (Institute of Electrical and Electronics Engineers Inc., New York, 1982). The first chapter of this book gives an excellent overview of speech/hearing function.

11 *I See What You Mean* (BBC Publications, 1975)

12 *Deafness*, John Ballantyne (Churchill Livingstone, 3rd edition 1977)

13 *Communication Barriers in the Elderly*, R.F. McCall (Age Concern, England, 1979)

14 *Choice of Habit*, Jack Vinten Fenton (MacDonald and Evans, London, 1973)

15 *Why Not Relax?* (Church's Council of Healing)

16 *Diseases of the Ear*, Stewart Mawson (Edward Arnold, London, 4th edition, 1979)

17 *Living with Giddiness*, M. Seiffert – leaflet produced by Link, The British Centre for Deafened People.